CULTURE AND POWER
IN THE CLASSROOM

Critical Studies in Education and Culture Series

CULTURE AND POWER IN THE CLASSROOM

A CRITICAL FOUNDATION FOR BICULTURAL EDUCATION

ANTONIA DARDER

Critical Studies in Education and Culture Series
edited by Henry A. Giroux and Paulo Freire

BERGIN & GARVEY
WESTPORT, CONNECTICUT • LONDON

Library of Congress Cataloging-in-Publication Data

Darder, Antonia.
    Culture and power in the classroom : a critical foundation for
bicultural education / Antonia Darder.
        p.   cm.—(Critical studies in education and culture)
    Includes bibliographical references and index.
    ISBN 0-89789-236-4 (hb. : alk. paper).—ISBN 0-89789-239-9 (pb.
alk. paper)
    1. Intercultural education—United States. 2. Educational
sociology—United States. 3. Educational equalization—United
States. 4. Education—Political aspects—United States.
5. Teaching.   I. Title. II. Series: Critical studies in education
& culture.
LB1099.3.D37   1991
370.19'0973—dc20   91-29793

British Library Cataloguing in Publication Data is available.

Library of Congress Catalog Card Number: 91-29793
ISBN: 0-89789-236-4 (HB)
        0-89789-239-9 (PB)

First published in 1991

Bergin & Garvey, 88 Post Road West, Westport, CT 06881
An imprint of Greenwood Publishing Group, Inc.

Printed in the United States of America

∞"

The paper used in this book complies with the
Permanent Paper Standard issued by the National
Information Standards Organization (Z39.48–1984).

P

In order to keep this title in print and available to the academic community, this edition
was produced using digital reprint technology in a relatively short print run. This would
not have been attainable using traditional methods. Although the cover has been changed
from its original appearance, the text remains the same and all materials and methods
used still conform to the highest book-making standards.

*To my children, Gabriel, Christy, and Kelly Flores,
who have taught me, above all, the true meaning
of love, struggle, commitment, and solidarity;
and to my father in the struggle, Paulo Freire,
who is a living example of these qualities.*

CONTENTS

FIGURES

SERIES FOREWORD

Antonia Darder's *Culture and Power in the Classroom* presents a passionate analysis of the pedagogical dimension of culture, particularly when she critically describes cultural experiences or the experiences of cultural subjects within a xenophobic context that too often treats difference with disrespect. Her book makes us confront the experience of cultural subjects that are not allowed to live a fully multicultural life in a society which is, by definition and make-up, multicultural. I say this with much conviction; I fear that most of these cultural subjects are living only a form of multicultural formality and not a substantive multicultural existence—to the extent that the U.S. cultural hegemony systematically relegates all forms of multicultural expression considered outside of the so-called "common culture" to the margins.

Darder describes the cultural experience of the "other" which also constitutes her own personal narrative, since she herself is a living testimony of cultural subjugation in a society that purports to be the model democracy. Her book provides us with important theoretical tools with which to deconstruct the colonial educational practice within the larger context of culture. By analyzing the structures of cultural dominance within the ever more present cultural hegemonic forces that now characterize the U.S. educational landscape, Darder unveils the very methods, practices, and raison d'etre of the colonialist educational ideology.

Her work is not merely a description of the colonial education practice that depreciates rather than affirms the lived experiences of cultural groups that have been sentenced to the margins of "democracy". It is also a courageous denunciation of antidemocratic practices.

When she passionately calls for a radical and critical pedagogy, Darder offers us pedagogical structures that are antagonistic to the colonial educational practices which function under the veil of democracy. She not only opts to cease being a make-believe cultural subject, but she also ruptures with her oppressive past and present experience in order to propose an educational alternative which, by its very nature and seriousness, must be radical and critical. Darder's book is not only scientifically correct, but it is also a book about dreams, a book that points to a necessary utopia for those who participate in the frustrating struggle for a more just and democratic education. That is, her book not only describes rigorously how the colonial ideology suffocates the voices of the "other", but it also provides us with a language of possibility. Darder inspires and challenges us to rethink what it means to live in a truly cultural democracy.

Paulo Freire

PREFACE

The theoretical foundation for this work is strongly influenced by the writings of Brazilian educator and philosopher Paulo Freire and American educational theorist Henry Giroux, in addition to the work of other theorists who, over the past thirty years, have addressed those issues related to subordinate cultural groups and the impact of dominant cultural forces on the lives of students from disenfranchised communities. True to its theoretical underpinnings, this book represents an effort to confront those dominant cultural values and practices that function in the schooling process to marginalize and silence the voices of Black, Latino, Asian, Native American and other bicultural students in the United States.

A primary purpose of this work is to articulate theoretical principles from which to develop a critical practice of bicultural education. It does not propose or provide instrumental formulas or recipes for duplication, imitation, or immediate execution of a specific model. Rather, it is an attempt to develop a new language by which bicultural educators may gain the perspective to evaluate their current practices with bicultural students and to formulate new directions in the interest of linking education with a pedagogy of differences. In essence, this work represents a pedagogy of possibilities—one that, above all, respects the capacity of teachers to redefine their roles as transformative intellectuals rather than simple dispensers of sterile and decomposing knowledge.

The need for such a pedagogy is crucial in light of the rapid shifts in demographics currently taking place in this country. If leading demographers are correct, by the turn of the century there will be an even greater number of geographical areas in the United States with populations that are primarily bicultural. Already, many of the nation's major urban centers, such as Los Angeles, San Francisco, Chicago, Miami, and New York, have school districts in which bicultural students comprise from 70 to 90 percent of all students enrolled.

Unfortunately, teachers in these districts are ill prepared to meet the needs of a majority of the children who enter their classrooms. This creates a twofold consequence, reflected first and foremost in the alarming statistics on attrition and dropout rates of bicultural students, and second in morale problems and high teacher attrition levels in these districts as well. This book attempts, in a small way, to address both these concerns through proposing a critical theoretical foundation that can specifically address the needs of bicultural students.

Throughout the text, the term *bicultural* is utilized instead of "minority"—a term that linguistically, and hence politically, reflects and perpetuates a view of subordinate cultures as deficient and disempowered. Bicultural, in this context, connotes an enculturation process that is distinct from that of monocultural Anglo-American students. This distinction is derived from the fact that bicultural students, throughout their development, must contend with: (1) two cultural systems whose values are very often in direct conflict; and (2) a set of sociopolitical and historical forces dissimilar to those of mainstream Anglo-American students and the educational institutions that bicultural students must attend. The term is also intended to project a more accurate picture of the worldview of students of color.

The term *cultural democracy* reflects the perspective and philosophy of Ramirez and Castaneda (1974). Specifically, it pertains to an educational philosophy that affirms the right of individuals to be educated in their own language and learning style and the right to maintain a bicultural identity—that is, to retain an identification with their culture of origin while integrating, in a constructive manner, the institutional values of the dominant culture. Further, this view argues for the necessity of institutional milieus, curricular materials, and educational approaches that are sensitive to the student's history, sociopolitical reality, and cultural orientation. While this definition represents only a starting point, the text to follow expands its scope to create a critical political construct for bicultural education.

Critical pedagogy refers to an educational approach rooted in the tradition of critical theory. Critical educators perceive their primary function as emancipatory and their primary purpose as commitment to creating the conditions for students to learn skills, knowledge, and modes of inquiry that will allow them to examine critically the role that society has played in their self-formation. More specifically, critical pedagogy is designed to give students the tools to examine how society has functioned to shape and constrain their aspirations and goals, and prevent them from even dreaming about a life outside the one they presently know (Giroux, 1981).

A major concern of critical pedagogy is that students develop the critical capacities to reflect, critique and act to transform the conditions under which they live. Further, critical pedagogy is one of the few educational perspectives that recognizes the need to develop a sensitivity to aspects of culture, although few projects that critically address the needs of bicultural students in the United States have been actualized. The critical foundation for bicultural education presented here represents only a partial step toward understanding the reality of bicultural students. It is offered in the hope that it will help generate a much-needed dialogue not yet a part of the discourse of public schooling. As such, it is meant to affirm openly and to support the emancipatory efforts of educators everywhere.

Finally, this book is an effort toward bringing to an end the historical educational neglect that continues to exist with respect to bicultural students. It is intended as a transformative intellectual act of empowerment that can be of service to those committed educators who struggle to overcome the consequences of this institutional neglect. But even more, it represents a political project of hope and possibility fueled by a faith in the collective power of human beings to struggle for freedom from the bondage of social oppression.

ACKNOWLEDGMENTS

I would like to express my thanks and deepest appreciation to Al Louch, Joe Weeres, and Scott Warren for their assistance during the beginning phases of this work; to my friend, comrade, and mentor, Henry Giroux, for his invaluable support and theoretical guidance; Connie Hurston and Makungu Akinyela for their friendship and the intellectual challenges we have faced together; to Laura Treister, who in the true spirit of friendship and solidarity prepared this manuscript; to Ernesto Salcedo for his kindness and support; and to my mother, Carmen Rodriguez, for the great love and courage she inspires in my life.

CHAPTER 1

THE PROBLEM WITH TRADITIONAL AMERICAN PEDAGOGY AND PRACTICE

> Any education given by a group tends to socialize its members, but the quality and value of the socialization depends upon the habits and aims of the group.
>
> John Dewey
> *Democracy and Education*

Historically, public education has been the only legitimate hope for escape from poverty for the majority of people of color. Contrary to the prevailing stereotypical notion that parents of color prevent their children from engaging successfully in educational pursuits, many of these parents actively encourage, urge, support, and struggle for their children to get an education. Many examples exist of parents who toiled long hours, sold prized possessions, and became heavily indebted for the sole purpose of assisting their children through college.

Yet despite these heroic efforts by parents and major community movements to improve the nature of education and create greater opportunities for bicultural[1] students, Black, Latino, Native American, and Asian students continue to fall through the cracks in alarming numbers. In major cities such as Los Angeles, San Francisco, Chicago, New York, and Miami, where bicultural students comprise from 70 to 90 percent of the student population, dropout rates of 50 percent and greater are the norm. Of those who manage to enroll in college, only a small percentage manage to complete degrees.[2]

What is the cause of this long history of underachievement among students of color, particularly when compared to their Anglo-American counterparts? Traditional attempts to address this question have engendered various and distinct points of view. One of the most persistent arguments in the field of education has been waged between two contrasting perspectives: *nature* (genetics) versus *nurture* (environment).

Those who view the problem as one of nature have been active in an effort to establish scientific proof that the primary cause of underachievement among bicultural students is related to a deficit in genetic traits. The work of James S. Coleman (1966) and Arthur Jensen (1969) has, directly or indirectly, functioned to support this notion. Proponents of the nature argument have, in general, also been well entrenched in a conservative educational ideology.

On the other side of the argument we find the nurture advocates (Miller, 1958; Bloom, 1964; Lewis, 1966; Moynihan, 1965; Cohen et al., 1968) who, for the most part, espouse a liberal view. From this perspective, the underachievement of bicultural students is considered to be primarily the result of the environment. Those who maintain a nurture argument readily point to the cycle of poverty, cultural deprivation, and the child's underprivileged environment as the fundamental cause of the problem. Hence, liberals quickly call for compensatory programs and reform efforts that will function to eliminate the debilitating effects that the home environment has had on bicultural students.

Although it may not seem apparent at first glance, both perspectives equally place the burden of responsibility for academic failure on the students' shoulders. Although the dynamics of victim-blaming are much more obvious within a conservative perspective, which clearly functions in support of the status quo, liberal victim-blaming functions in a more hidden and subtle manner. Although liberals, in essence, recognize that inequity exists in American society, they seek solutions that will work to prepare (change) the bicultural student so that she or he will be able to compete better in the (unequal) system.

Yet, after twenty years of liberal reforms and compensatory educational programs, problems of educational and income inequities stubbornly persist, with less than 10 percent of low-income students of color ever moving out of the lower social stratum. Of those who do, most only move a few short steps up the social mobility scale (deLone, 1979). Meanwhile, the great liberal hopes of ameliorating the inequities of the system have turned sour as liberal influences continue to lose momentum in the midst of a neo-conservative movement that gained momentum and prominence through the support of former Secretary of Education William Bennett. Why have liberal educational reforms failed to correct the effects of environmental forces that produce inequality in schools? Are conservative theories of natural intelligence and their notion of genetic intellectual deficiency valid? Or has the etiology of the problem in both views been fundamentally misdiagnosed?

In considering these questions, it is significant to note again that conservatives and liberals alike have consistently identified the cause and the problem within the student. Either the bicultural student is considered to be genetically inferior or environmentally inferior, but nonetheless the cause and problem is inherent in the student. It is particularly revealing that neither view has ever seriously challenged or placed responsibility for the underachievement of bicultural students directly on the traditional educational values and practices that structure relationships in schools.

Hence, if we are to move toward effective strategies to promote the academic success of bicultural students, we must begin by asking this fundamental question: How does traditional American pedagogy perpetuate the underachievement of students of color? Through an analysis of those values that inform American educational theories and practices, we can begin to understand better how particular views perpetuate inequity and function systematically to oppress bicultural students in this country.

A CRITIQUE OF TRADITIONAL AMERICAN PEDAGOGY

Traditional American pedagogy generally has been divided into two perspectives: conservative and liberal. Both these views essentially uphold the notion that the object of education is the free, enterprising, independent individual, and that students should be educated in order to adapt to the existing configurations of power that make up the dominant society.

Conservatives are, for the most part, intent on maintaining the system as is. Any changes should be considered very carefully and implemented very slowly. Liberals, on the other hand, do recognize inequities in the system and the need for change, but they believe that the American capitalist system is fundamentally superior and that it can function effectively with a few modifications by way of compensatory programs and reform policies. It is interesting to note that these reform programs are often perceived by many conservatives as the cause of social problems when the reforms fail to yield their promised outcomes. This is particularly true in respect to the educational concerns that relate to bicultural students. In order to understand the long-term effects of these two traditional views on bicultural communities, it is helpful to turn for a moment to the specific values that engender each perspective.

1. Valores implícitos —

Conservative Educational Discourse

Central to the very nature of a conservative educational discourse is the implicit purpose of conserving the social and economic status quo through the perpetuation of institutional values and relationships that safeguard dominant power structures. Hence a major emphasis of such an ideology, by necessity, is related to basic values of uniformity, consensus, and ethnocentrism. Without the people's consensus and uniformity of belief in the existing nature of democracy, and the unquestioning superiority of the dominant culture's worldview, many of the currently existing dominant power structures might long ago have become an endangered species in the United States.

A prominent value that clearly supports different forms of cultural oppression (i.e., classism, racism, and sexism) and that is widely reinforced by a conservative educational discourse is that of the existing hierarchical structure of society. It is precisely the acceptance of this social view that functions to guarantee that, for the most part, students from the dominant culture end up at

[handwritten marginalia: "nota contrabar", "Estudiantes", "Blancos", "minorias"]

the top of the hierarchy, and students from the subordinate cultures end up at the bottom. In the United States, as in all capitalist societies, the most politically powerful are those who control the bulk of society's resources,[3] including the military and state apparatuses. This economic and institutional control is clearly perpetuated from generation to generation through the process of schooling, which is defined by the dominant society as a source of status. As such, the dominant culture strives systematically to control the structure of schooling and to ensure that its children are clearly placed in secure positions of power to enter controlling roles in American society.

Samuel Bowles and Herbert Gintes (1976) argue that the social hierarchy is not only maintained along divisions of cognitive skills, but—even more importantly—along noncognitive or behavioral skills that are directly related to social class. These skills, which are differentially reinforced by different schools and among students in the same educational environments, are most significant in relation to what students learn regarding their appropriate future roles in society. This is evident in the nature of behaviors that are rewarded in upper-class students (i.e., aggressiveness, original thinking, etc.) and those passive or allegedly civilized behaviors rewarded in bicultural students. Although it is clear that a colonizing knowledge is imparted to both, it is far more detrimental in its consequences to the lives of bicultural students, who comprise a disproportionately larger number of the lower classes. Martin Carnoy views this process in the following manner:

[handwritten marginalia: "un solo punto de vista"]

Learning in public schools is organized to maintain the hierarchical structure. Children do not learn about their environment from the perspective of their own reality, but from the white wealthy view. Thus, poverty, drug addiction, and crime are an individual failing rather than the result of an inequitable and racist economy; children are taught to compete for the limited "top" positions in society rather than working together to improve their collective condition. (Carnoy, 1974, p. 365)

Thus, bicultural students are socialized to perceive their place in society within a hierarchical structure that is informed by values that benefit the dominant culture. As such, schools, as well as other social institutions, produce and interpret knowledge that serves as a silencing agent, in that it relegates greater legitimacy to the abstract reality developed by this knowledge than the actual daily experiences that shape students' lives. This hierarchical socialization is then further reinforced by the fact that success or failure in school is considered an individual responsibility. When bicultural students perform poorly, it is clearly considered the students' fault. The fact that the opportunities to succeed in the dominant culture are unequally distributed is ignored in the context of a traditional educational discourse. This individualization of responsibility serves effectively to diffuse class and race identity and interclass/race hostility. As such, it effectively provides an acceptable justification for the unequal distribution of resources in American society.

American schools strongly reinforce an acceptance of differential roles in the economy and society as a just and democratic way of organizing social relations. In this manner, the class system of education provides an effective vehicle for the dominant culture to *civilize* bicultural populations to ensure that society remains orderly and safe. As such, the dominant culture is able to maintain its status of privilege and power over society and its institutions.

In an effort to understand how these values function, it is worth noting that, for the large majority of bicultural students, schooling in the United States is structured to limit individual choice by defining well-specified and uncreative roles in the social and economic hierarchy. Schooling defines students' potential for them on the basis of the hierarchy's needs, while ignoring the needs of students. Schooling for a hierarchical structure is therefore a colonizing device. It may change the types of choices that individuals from subordinated cultures can have, but nonetheless it serves essentially to limit the control bicultural students can ultimately have over their own lives (Bowles & Gintes, 1976).

The conservative educational discourse is also deeply entrenched in a *positivist* ideology: a view of the world that is clearly governed by an instrumentally technocratic rationality that glorifies a logic and method based on the natural sciences. With its emphasis on technical knowledge, it enforces an empirical analytical method of inquiry that incorporates the notion of quantifiable objective facts and neutral observation. Henry Giroux elaborates on the values that engender this "culture of positivism"[4] in American schools:

In this view, knowledge is objective . . . classroom knowledge is often treated as an external body of information, the production of which appears to be independent of human beings. From this perspective, objective knowledge is viewed as independent of time and place; it becomes universalized, ahistorial knowledge. Moreover, it is expressed in a language that is basically technical and allegedly value-free. . . . Knowledge, then, becomes not countable and measurable, it also becomes impersonal. Teaching in this pedagogical paradigm is usually discipline-based and treats subject matter in a compartmentalized and automized fashion. (Giroux, 1981, p. 52)

This conservative discourse often functions to promote passivity among bicultural students through its adherence to a view of knowledge as objective, separate, and devoid of the knowing subject. A major underlying assumption that supports this perspective is based on the notion that there exists a dichotomy between human beings and the world. As a consequence, students are trapped into reductionist behavioral definitions, while learning is reduced to the transmission of predefined knowledge. This view is clearly inherent in what Paulo Freire describes as a "banking" system of education, which incorporates a fundamentally "narrative" character:

It involves a narrating subject (the teacher) and patient, listening objects (the students). The contents, whether values or empirical dimensions of reality, tend in the process to become lifeless and petrified. . . . [T]he teacher talks about reality as if it were motionless, static, compartmentalized, and predictable. Or else, he [or she] expounds on a topic completely alien to the existential experience of the student. (Freire, 1970, p. 57)

The technocratic interests that inform dominant educational discourses are based on a view of knowledge that perpetuates an acceptance of submission to laws governing the technical mastery of human beings and nature. This is particularly apparent in the instrumental definition of *theory* as a scientific framework for the manipulation of the environment with the purpose of accomplishing a particular state of affairs or preventing its occurrence. It is this logic, with its emphasis on control, prediction, and certainty, that permits the disregard of historical consciousness, particularly as it relates to subordinate cultures, the negation of human agency through the systematic silencing of student voices, and an educational structure of dominance that fundamentally functions to support the needs of the existing power relations and their corresponding social formations (Giroux, 1981).

A final characteristic that supports the inequity in American schools is the traditional, uncritical acceptance of the existing relationship between schools and the larger society. Schools are viewed as neutral and apolitical institutions whose sole purpose is to educate students with the necessary knowledge and skills to render them functional in (and to) society. It is this basic lack of inquiry into the relationship between schools and society that permits the structure and ideology of the dominant culture to be rendered unproblematic and the oppressive contradictions inherent in this view to remain concealed within the mainstream educational process (Aronowitz & Giroux, 1985).

Liberal Educational Discourse

In contrast to the positivist rationality that informs traditional conservative pedagogy, a liberal educational discourse strongly incorporates the central pedagogical themes of appropriation, subjectivity, and intentionality, along with a strong humanistic emphasis on the uniqueness of the individual. True to its hermeneutic principles, a liberal educational perspective regards the student as an active participant in the learning process who is constantly negotiating and renegotiating knowledge and meaning with others in a mutual effort to produce and define the constitutive rules that shape and mold their relationships and interactions with their world. Giroux elaborates on this interpretive view of knowledge:

Instead of seeing school knowledge as objective and value-free, it was seen as a social constitution tied to the interests, perceptions, and experiences of those who produce and negotiate its meaning. Instead of teachers and students acting as agents of received values and truths, they were now viewed as producers of values and truths. As knowledge became relativized, modes of pedagogy developed that stressed experiences and interpersonal relations. (Giroux, 1981, p. 12)

Pluralismo:

The liberal educational discourse also traditionally has embraced a philosophy of pluralism, which argues for a political ideal of equality and justice. The inherent contradiction in this perspective arises from a failure to recognize the fundamental inequalities that exist in American society. "Pluralism ignores the tension between political democracy and economic inequality. That is, it fails to acknowledge that equality of opportunity and the importance of human reflectiveness may be impeded by particularistic private interests in the economic sphere that use the state to impose severe constraints on certain segments of the population" (Giroux, 1983, p. 189). With its one-sided subjective notion of political participation and decision-making, pluralism results in a deeply flawed political ideal that consequently does little to change the institutional conditions that perpetuate the oppression of subordinate cultures in the United States.

Further, it is fundamentally this disregard for the basic nature of existing social relationships in the wider society that permits liberal educators to fall into the trap of victim-blaming. With its heavy reliance on subjective consciousness and a descriptive orientation, the traditional liberal discourse is stripped of the criteria necessary for critically evaluating the various interpretations of the existing social, cultural, economic, and political reality.

evaluar   *más abierto*

This is particularly evident in the environmental interpretation of cognitive development traditionally utilized by liberal educators to explain the underachievement of bicultural students. This view encompasses the assumption that inequality of social standing reflects inequality of individual capability—a natural conclusion, given the liberal emphasis on the individual. Thus, those environmental forces that are considered significant to the cognitive development of mainstream Anglo-American values are examined within bicultural communities to determine what could be the problem. Studies based on this view invariably determine that bicultural children do not receive enough verbal and social stimulation in their homes; consequently—it is concluded—the children develop low verbal ability, which hinders their school performance.

Richard deLone (1979) identifies the following variations on this environmental theme so often voiced by liberal educators:

debido a que los padres no pueden crear condiciones para aumentar sus conocimientos en casa — resultado Tienen problemas en la escuela.

Ustedula fam. mexicana.

[Bicultural] children grow up in intellectually and verbally barren, "culturally deprived" homes, where they fail to receive enough stimulation from their parents to develop cognitive skills necessary to succeed in school and adulthood.

[Bicultural] and working-class parents have rigid and authoritarian childrearing styles, which limit the stimulation their children receive and suppress the playfulness and natural curiosity that full cognitive development requires.

Consecuen-cia de ser Pobre   Poverty creates its own culture, a culture of instant gratification, sexual promiscuity, and disorder, and the social and emotional development of children who grow up in this culture equips them poorly for success in schools or adulthood.

[Bicultural] children belong to subcultures the norms, values, and styles of which differ from those of the dominant society and this difference makes it hard for them to cope with schools or ultimately the work requirements of the dominant society. (deLone, 1979, p. 127)

Sin estimularlos en la niñez

Each of these views also incorporates a more general theory of *childhood determinism*, which argues that adult intelligence and social and emotional competencies are critically shaped during the early years. This has supported the liberal educational reform tradition that dictates early childhood intervention (e.g., the Headstart program), in spite of the fact that there is no strong empirical evidence to support this theory (deLone, 1979). It is also important to note that, by espousing a liberal theory of childhood determinism and cultural deprivation, educational institutions have been permitted to function within a conceptual framework that serves to absolve schools from responsibility for the widespread underachievement of bicultural students. Hence, it has permitted the dynamics of victim-blaming to overshadow the necessity for systemic change and to distract attention from the basic causes of inequality while leaving the primary social injustices untouched (Ryan, 1976).

In many respects, the problem with a liberal educational discourse is that it falls into the ideological trap resulting from a dichotomized view of the world. While the conservative perspective disempowers students through its insistence on an objective and neutral view of knowledge, the liberal discourse commits a similar offense in reverse. With its heavy emphasis on individual subjectivity, it fails to move beyond a relativistic notion of knowledge and hence disregards the ideological and structural constraints of the dominant culture that inform school practices, which function to the detriment of many students of color.

It is precisely this theoretical neglect that hinders the liberal educator's ability to understand how meanings are maintained or how they might distort rather than illuminate reality. Consequently, in spite of its humanistic posture, the traditional liberal discourse also degenerates into an ahistorical, undialectical, and apolitical view that functions ultimately to curtail the forms of critical thinking and constructive dialogue that could lead to a critical and productive education for bicultural students.

CRITIQUE OF TRADITIONAL EDUCATIONAL PRACTICES

Any critique of U.S. schools would be incomplete without an examination of the educational practices that are informed by traditional pedagogical values. Various educational practices, in particular, have contributed to the underachievement of bicultural students. The effects of these practices are better understood by looking at the manner in which public schools have utilized a combination of meritocracy, intelligence testing, tracking and ability grouping, teacher expectations, and the curriculum to perpetuate inequality in the United States.

Meritocracy

Meritocracy refers to an educational practice whereby the talented are chosen and moved ahead on the basis of their achievement. The talented, for the most part, are members of the dominant culture whose values comprise the very foundations that inform the knowledge and skills a student must possess or achieve to be designated as an individual who merits reward. The blind spot in this practical system of advancement is that, while in reality it is schooling as a cultural and historical process in which select groups are positioned within asymmetrical relations of power on the basis of specific race, class, and gender groups, it sees itself rather as stemming from a process of schooling that is value free and neutral. Peter McLaren (1988) elaborates further on the tautologous character of meritocracy in American schools: "To argue that schools are meritocratic institutions is a conceptual tautology: successful learners are those whom schools reward. . . . Missing from this logic is a recognition that students from White, affluent backgrounds are privileged over other groups, not on the basis of merit but because of the advantage that comes with having money and increased social status" (p. 163).

Meritocracy constitutes a form of systematic control by which the dominant culture controls the structure of schooling and secures for its children positions of power in society. Public schools persistently legitimize this myth of meritocracy to guarantee that successful participation in the educational system becomes the visible process by which individuals are allocated or rewarded with higher social status. Through a system of merit, the process of unequal privilege and entitlement is successfully smokescreened under the guise of democratic selection.

The perpetuation of this educational system of rewards for individual achievement plays a primary role in the reproduction and reinforcement of a hierarchically structured labor force, which is designed to keep in place the inequality of the status quo. Bowles and Gintes describe this particular function of schooling:

Schools legitimate inequality through the ostensibly meritocratic manner by which they reward and promote students, and allocate them to distinct positions in the occupational hierarchy. They create and reinforce patterns of social class, racial, and sexual identification among students which allow them to relate "properly" to their eventual standing in the hierarchy of authority and status in the production process. Schools foster types of personal development compatible with the relationship of dominance and subordination in the economic sphere. (Bowles and Gintes, 1976, p. 11)

This function is more concretely reflected in the manner in which students are awarded degrees and credentialed for their successful participation in the educational system. These educational credentials, in turn, function to demonstrate an individual possesses the legitimate cultural capital that prospective employers and the society at large will recognize as adequate preparation, which then entitles the individual to occupational status. Consequently, as credentials have clearly become the essential ticket that determines whether an individual may gain access to jobs, goods, or economic security, the role schools play in the process of social domination is widely expanded (Aronowitz & Giroux, 1985).

Further, the U.S. public school system, with its guarantee of social mobility (if only a student can demonstrate the right combination of innate intelligence, cognitive development, motivation, and drive), functions as a twofold justification of the dominant culture for explaining the unequal distribution of wealth in this country. On the one hand, it establishes the merit of the dominant culture as the main criterion for achieved social position; and on the other hand, it persists in blaming bicultural students for their underachievement by implying that they do not have the necessary intelligence, motivation, and/or drive to partake of the educational opportunities so readily offered them by a system of free public education.

Intelligence Testing Proebes.

The utilization of intelligence testing in the schools historically has played an insidious role in the perpetuation of underachievement among bicultural students. This is apparent in the fact that all forms of intelligence testing have traditionally incorporated a technically instrumental view of knowledge, emphasizing an empirical methodology to measure student achievement. This has resulted in the construction of testing instruments as value-free scientific tools that are considered to result in objective, measurable, and quantifiable data. As such, the predefined knowledge and skills tested have been given priority at the expense of the knowledge and experience students bring with them to the classroom. It is this educational positivism that fuels the continued evaluation of bicultural students based on intelligence quotients, reading scores, and the other forms of standardized test results, which are then utilized to sort, regulate, and control students and their subsequent achievement in American schools (McLaren, 1988).

Intelligence quotient (IQ) scores, in particular, have been the means by which schools have rationalized student selection procedures to make them appear more democratic and to conceal their role in sustaining the hierarchical nature of society. IQ measures have been used consistently as a means to secure acceptance of an individual's allotted place in society; and in this respect, IQ testing has functioned clearly as a political enterprise of the dominant culture while masquerading in the guise of an objective and scientific measure of innate intelligence. Liam Hudson (1972), writing about IQ testing in *Race and Intelligence*, states, "The use of IQ tests has in fact taken on many of the qualities of a mystic rite. The IQ has come to be seen as a measurement that not merely summarizes the individual's capacity to perform tasks, but one which, in some unspecified way, puts a number to his [or her] essential worth" (p. 15).

Study after study reveals that children from the dominant culture do far better on IQ tests than bicultural children. Hence, if one accepts the notion that IQ tests are in fact a measure of native intelligence, then it would be logical that Anglo-American children must be considered to have more innate intelligence than members of bicultural groups. This view, whose focus has been the relationship of heredity and intelligence, has never gone without advocates, as evidenced in the work of the father of psychometrics, Francis Galton (1869), and more recently in the work of Arthur R. Jensen (1969) and others.

What such an analysis lacks, however, is a recognition of the ideological paradigm that engenders this view and the social conditions that permit its perpetuation. It follows the Darwinist—and consequent Galtonian—notions of a ladder view of society with the climbers moving with different weights given to them at the start of their journey preordaining the final result of the competition (Daniels & Houghton, 1972). It is this conservative notion of the survival of the fittest and its view of the dominant culture as the fittest, without concern for the social and economic context of inequality, that supports the perpetuation of a hierarchical structure of society.

In spite of arguments to the contrary by many conservative educational advocates, IQ testing is unable to function as a fair measurement of innate intelligence, because its primary concern is directly linked to a relative ranking of people based on criteria derived solely from the values of a selective cultural system.

Further, intelligence quotients clearly represent a tradition that has judged intelligence according to what the tests test, and high intelligence as related to doing well in school—two variables that are ideologically inseparable and fully permeated by the values of the ruling class. As such, intelligence testing has been responsible for creating the disease it was intended to cure, while in turn it produces the rationalization that students who fail ought to fail (Richardson & Spears, 1972).

Tracking and Ability Grouping

Tracking is defined as "any school selection system that attempts to homogenize classroom placements in terms of students' personal qualities, performances, or aspirations. Tracking is also a general term that includes both ability grouping and curriculum grouping and which places an emphasis upon social similarities" (Rosenbaum, 1976). Often, this form of grouping may involve the temporary placement of children by ability or interest in a particular classroom, or may involve the grouping of an entire school.

The public school system, through its consistent use of tracking and ability grouping, has perpetuated a caste system in which the majority of children of low-income status leave school solely prepared to enter society at the same low-income levels as their parents (Carter, 1970). This mechanism, which acts primarily as a sorting device, historically has supported and reinforced attitudes and practices that result in the unfair treatment of bicultural students.

The relationship between the tracking process and intelligence testing is a fundamental one to American education. From the beginning, ability grouping and track placement have relied heavily on IQ and standardized test scores to assign student educational placement. In addition, there is strong evidence to suggest that teacher recommendations and the students' race and social class also have played a major role in determining student assignments. Consequently, due to inadequate testing and other variables such as teacher bias and inadequate knowledge pertaining to the developmental needs of bicultural children, tracking systems have usually assigned a highly disproportionate number of bicultural students into low-ability groups, as compared to Anglo-American students (Knowles & Prewitt, 1969; Suarez, 1978).

From both a statistical and a historical standpoint, it is significant to note that the curriculum content, type of instruction, degree of selection, frequency and type of teacher–student interaction, and available educational resources all tend to favor higher over lower tracks. Since tracking practices so often do result in racial and economic homogeneity within classrooms, these differences in content and experience can also help to explain the underachievement of bicultural students in American schools (Persell, 1977).

Bowles and Gintes (1976) argue that the tracking system is found at all levels of education. Schools, colleges, and universities reflect a stratified multitiered system that is dominated by the Ivy League institutions, followed by less prestigious schools, colleges, and universities, and ending with poor urban schools and community colleges. What this system also tends to reflect is both the social status of the families of the students and the hierarchy of work relationships into which each type of student will move after graduation. In *Schooling in Capitalist America*, Bowles and Gintes describe how this process works:

The segregation of students not destined for the top has allowed the development of procedures and curricula more appropriate to their future "needs", as defined by their actual occupational opportunities. The vast majority of students in [public schools] and community colleges are programmed for failure. Great efforts are made—through testing and counseling—to convince students that their lack of success is objectively attributable to their own inadequacies . . . Bringing students' hopes into line with the realities of the job market is facilitated by [the] tracking system. (Bowles & Gintes, 1976, p. 211)

Tracking has played, without a doubt, a critical role in the underachievement of bicultural students. Many studies in the field strongly indicate that tracking and ability grouping function to build confidence in a few chosen students, at the expense of the self-concept[5] and formal educational development of a large proportion of the student population—a population that is disproportionately represented by bicultural students. This structural feature of tracking is considered to socialize the students exposed to it so that those in lower tracks come to feel and perceive themselves as deserving less from life, while those in higher tracks come to expect more. It is in this way that tracking and ability grouping influence achievement, self-concept, and attitudes, via both teacher expectations and student internalization of these experiences. Hence, the outcome of tracking can be correlated with the substantial inequality in society and also suggests how these inequalities become accepted by the society at large (Persell, 1977).

Teacher Expectations

As suggested in the previous discussion, the tracking process is heavily mediated by teacher expectations, and many studies have been conducted that demonstrate the effect that teachers' expectations have on the children in their classrooms (Clark, 1965; Rosenthal & Jacobson, 1968; Rist, 1977; Glasgow, 1980). These findings generally have indicated that, where children are perceived as bright, articulate, and motivated, the children fulfill the prophecy of success. Where children are perceived as slow, dull, and unmotivated, they reproduce the behavior and attitudes that support negative teacher expectations (Ryan, 1981).

In assessing the impact of teacher expectations on bicultural students, it is important to understand what Caroline H. Persell (1977) calls the "genesis of teacher expectations." The genesis of teacher expectations involves a number of essential factors. First, it includes the social context, which incorporates the prevailing social attitudes associated with race, class structure, and the social, political, and economic ideology. Second, teacher expectations are influenced by the specific pedagogical theories and conceptual frameworks, as well as educational structures and practices, instilled by teacher training programs. This category reflects the climate of expectations surrounding testing, tracking, and record-keeping. Third, crucial in the development of teacher expectations are the teacher's personal experiences related to race, education, and peer socialization. And fourth, teacher expectations are found to be significantly influenced by student characteristics such as race, class, appearance, behavior, and test performance.

What is particularly significant is that the sorting process that results from teachers' expectations functions primarily as an unconscious mechanism, which helps to explain its hegemonic function and its resistance to change. Hence, teacher expectations related to lower-class and bicultural students can result in any of the following consequences:

1. Teachers are more likely to hold negative expectations for lower-class and [bicultural] children than for middle-class white children.
2. Teacher expectations are affected by testing and tracking, procedures which are themselves biased against lower-class and [bicultural] children.
3. It is precisely such negative information that . . . suggests [it] is more potent in its consequences than positive expectations.
4. Expectations are related to teacher behaviors and to student cognitive changes even when IQ and achievement are controlled.
5. Given the less powerful position of lower-class and [bicultural] children in society, they appear to be more influenced by teacher expectations. (Persell, 1977, p. 132)

In looking at the results of teacher expectations, Rosenbaum (1976) places a strong emphasis on the question of how teachers' expectations determine the manner in which they allocate attention in the classroom. He argues that the most important teacher bias is related to this distribution of attention. Teachers report that they prepare more for college-track than noncollege-track classes, and they feel that lower-track business and general-track classes are so undemanding as to require little or no preparation at all. Lower-track students also report this same form of classroom treatment, noting that some lower-track teachers give a workbook assignment each day and then spend the class time ignoring students and reading the newspaper.

William Ryan (1981) strongly argues that teacher expectations and the subsequent attention that students receive or fail to receive influence greatly their level of achievement in the classroom. He says recent studies

have shown that, even when there is little substantial difference in the quantity of interaction between high-expectancy and low-expectancy groups, the qualitative differences are great. With students of whom they hold high expectations, teachers more often praise correct answers or "sustain" the interaction if the answer is incorrect—that is, they repeat or rephrase the question, give a clue, and in general try to get the student to continue to work toward a correct response. With pupils of whom they expect little, teachers are more inclined to accept correct answers with minimal praise and criticize incorrect answers. In addition, the teacher is much more likely to limit her [or his] interactions with these students to matters of class organization and discipline. (Ryan, 1976, p. 134)

As observed earlier by Persell (1977), bicultural students who find themselves at the bottom rungs of the social ladder are more likely to be influenced by teacher expectations than those from the upper and middle classes. As a consequence, bicultural students are much more likely to have their achievement negatively affected by negative teacher expectations. Further, this consciously or unconsciously reinforced social structure of dominance is intensified by various interrelated and cumulative processes that function together to depress the academic achievement of the majority of bicultural students, while supporting the educational success of students from the dominant culture.

The Curriculum

Curriculum traditionally refers to the coursework offered or required by an educational institution for the successful completion of a degree or credentialing objective. What constitutes its content is, for the most part, directly related to what form of knowledge and content is recognized as legitimate and necessary by those who dictate curricular decisions. These decisions strongly embody the values, attitudes, and biases inherent in the educational discourse of those who design and ultimately approve curriculum. Hence, the underlying principles related to both curriculum content and teaching methodology are derived from what is considered to be the function of education in American society: namely, the perpetuation of values and social relations that produce and legitimate the dominant worldview at the expense of a vast number of citizens.

This can be better understood by examining the neo-conservative movement's answer to educational reform. Two such major efforts include the call for *back-to-basics education* and state-mandated *teacher-proof curriculum*. Both represent models strongly steeped in an instrumental language that defines education basically as technically objective and value free. Within these approaches, classroom knowledge is viewed "as independent of human beings and as independent of time and place; it becomes universalized, ahistorical knowledge"—deceptively camouflaging the curriculum's hidden motivations (Giroux, 1983).

The common utilization of *behavioral objectives* as a framework for curriculum development and implementation in American schools reflects a search for certainty and technical control of knowledge and behavior. This is demonstrated clearly in its overemphasis on classroom management procedures, necessity, and efficiency, and on how-to techniques that inform educational approaches essentially geared to meet the logic of market demands. Students are taught in public schools primarily in terms of a set of prescribed techniques that will produce results and methodologies that are at once fragmented, antitheoretical, and skills oriented (Aronowitz & Giroux, 1985).

It is precisely through this adherence to a positivist educational perspective, with its emphasis on consensus, social conformity, and stability, that permits the perpetuation of the dominant culture through the *hidden curriculum*. Stanley Aronowitz and Henry Giroux describe how the hidden curriculum functions in public schools:

The dominant school culture functions not only to legitimate the interests and values of dominant groups; it also functions to marginalize and disconfirm knowledge forms and experiences that are extremely important to subordinate and oppressed groups. This can be seen in the way in which school curricula often ignore the histories of women, racial minorities, and the working class. . . . Schools legitimate dominant forms of culture through the hierarchically arranged bodies of knowledge that make up the curriculum as well as the way in which certain forms of linguistic capital and the individual (rather than collective) appropriation of knowledge is rewarded in schools. (Aronowitz & Giroux, 1985, pp. 147–48)

Curriculum texts, workbooks, manuals, films, and other artifacts utilized in American classrooms clearly produce meaning and define what is appropriate in social relations for students. This is evidenced by results gathered by recent content-analysis studies. One such study concluded that social studies books used in public schools are dominated by themes that support values of the dominant culture. These themes include the following: (1) an overvaluing of social harmony, social compromise, and political consensus, with very little said about social struggle or class conflict; (2) an intense nationalism and chauvinism; (3) a near-exclusion of labor history; and (4) a number of myths regarding the nature of political, economic, and social life (Anyon, 1980).

Through what curriculum excludes, as much as by what it includes, students are socialized into particular structures of society that benefit the dominant culture. Even where curriculum content has been altered or revised through liberal attempts at curriculum reform, teachers seldom move beyond their stereotypical perceptions of students based on class and color. Keddie's (1971) work illustrates this disparity in teacher attitudes. "Working-class students were taught how to follow rules, which usually meant learning how not to ask questions or raise issues that challenged teacher assumptions. . . . [M]iddle-class students were offered more complex treatments of class material, and their personal involvement in the class was endorsed rather than discouraged" (Giroux, 1985, p. 51).

Given this critique of traditional American pedagogy and its practices, it is highly evident that a lack of critical inquiry into the values informing traditional perspectives has resulted in school practices that prevent bicultural students from understanding their world—silencing their voices and relegating them to positions of powerlessness in American society. Hence, it is impossible to impact significantly the underachievement of bicultural students without addressing the issue of power in society and its role in the cultural subordination of people of color, in spite of proclaimed democratic ideals. It is this link between culture and power that must be challenged in any effort to develop a theory of critical bicultural education that can genuinely function toward the emancipatory interests of bicultural students in the United States.

NOTES

1. As noted in the Preface, the term *bicultural* is utilized here instead of "minority," specifically to designate students who identify themselves as Black, Latino, Chicano, Asian, Philipino, Native American Indian, and so forth.

2. An example of this phenomenon is illustrated by statistics on conferred degrees published by the University of California Admissions and Outreach Services in the 1988 edition of *Information Digest*. The following figures reflect the highly disproportionate percentage of advanced degrees conferred on Anglo-American students, as compared to bicultural students:

Degree Conferred	Anglo-American	Bicultural
High School	62%	38%
Bachelor's	71	29
Master's	84	16
Doctorate	86	14

These percentages are particularly disturbing in light of kindergarten-to-twelfth-grade enrollment figures, which indicate an almost equal number of Anglo-American (51%) and bicultural (49%) students enrolled statewide.

3. The *American Profile Poster* published by Pantheon Books in 1986 indicates that data on economic distribution of wealth in the United States demonstrate the following: More than 90 percent of all the net wealth is controlled by 10 percent of the population; 64 percent of the wealth is controlled by less than 1 percent of the population; and less than 10 percent of the country's net wealth is distributed among 90 percent of the population whose income ceiling is $85,000. The majority of the bicultural population is found in the bottom stratum of this 90-percent figure. The chart was constructed from data taken from U.S. government reports. The primary document was *Current Population Reports*.

4. It is important to note that Giroux (1981) is not referring to a particular philosophy of positivism, of which there are many complex, historically constructed strands. Instead, what he is referring to here is a *culture* of positivism as a constellation of ideological assumptions that support a technocratic view of the world.

5. In any discussion relating to the self-concept and/or self-esteem of bicultural students, it is significant to note there exists a number of studies (Valentine, 1971; McAdoo, 1977; 1978; Cross, Porter & Washington, 1979)

that strongly challenge the validity of the essentially monocultural criteria utilized in earlier studies to assess the self-concept/self-esteem of bicultural children. Although most of the major work in the field has focused on Black children, there is sufficient indication that assessment of self-concept/self-esteem in other bicultural children would also yield similar results under similar conditions. Also worth noting is the need for critical research with subordinate cultural groups that would specifically examine the differences in self-concept and/or self-esteem among bicultural individuals as they move back and forth from primary cultural environments (e.g., home, church, cultural events, etc.) to monocultural (Anglo) institutional environments (e.g., schools, government offices, occupational and professional settings, etc.).

CHAPTER 2

THE LINK BETWEEN CULTURE AND POWER

Democracy cannot be achieved without understanding power itself, how it is exerted, and where it lies.

Anthony Arblaster
Democracy

The primary purpose of this chapter is to examine the relationship between culture and power as a fundamental step toward the development of a critical foundation for bicultural education in the United States. Through an understanding of the nature of this relationship in American society, educators can begin to examine the power relations in classrooms that ultimately result in the subordination of bicultural students. And it is only through an examination of the link between culture and power that a critical theory of cultural democracy can emerge to function in creating the conditions that will support the emancipatory interests of students of color by incorporating their voices into the discourse of public schooling.

TRADITIONAL DEFINITIONS OF CULTURE

Much of the problem of understanding culture and its relationship to pedagogical theories and practices results from a failure to examine culture beyond those constructs that have been set forth by a Western anthropological discourse. Consequently, from this perspective, *culture* has traditionally been defined as being an all-embracing neutral category (Giroux, 1983). The result has been a multitude of research (Tyler, 1891; Boas, 1938; Mead, 1937; Whorf, 1956; Kluckhohn & Strodbeck, 1961; Cole & Scribner, 1974; Witkin & Berry, 1975; Munroe & Munroe, 1975) based on the expressed intent of delving into the question of cultural differences.

More specifically, these studies have treated cultural values as an inventory of discrete, equally important (neutral) phenomena, or as a complex that includes knowledge, belief, art, morals, laws, customs, and any other capacities and habits acquired by humans as members of society. The cultural data collected by many anthropologists and sociologists may be classified into four commonly utilized categories: (1) cultural values or value orientation, (2) heritage and cultural artifacts, (3) language, and (4) cognitive styles. Within these categories, life stages have been examined; the affective behavior of the group has been studied; sex roles have been defined; and values significant to Western culture—such as competitiveness, aggression, achievement, social motivation, and self-orientation—have been compared.

What is readily apparent from the standpoint of any critical analysis of much of this work is the obvious absence of specific reference to the issue of power and its relationship to the nature in which cultural relationships are structured and perpetuated within and between groups. Hence, educators have most often been involved with definitions of culture derived from a scientific rationality that is individualistic, apolitical, ahistorical, and based on a positivist notion of value-free inquiry and interpretation. At other times, attempts to counter this view have resulted in studies that are clouded by a humanistic relativism that ultimately fails, in the same manner, to question and challenge the issue of power and its role in shaping the cultural reality and worldview that groups hold. Henry Giroux (1988a) addresses this separation of culture from relations of power: "Culture in this view becomes the object of sociological inquiry and is analyzed primarily as an artifact that embodies and expresses the traditions and values of diverse groups. There is no attempt in this view to understand

culture as the shared and lived principles of life, characteristic
of different groups and classes as these emerge within asymmetrical relations of power and fields of struggle" (pp. 97–98).

(DOMINATION)
POWER AND TRUTH

Given the implicit conservative discourse that underlies the
value-free and neutral assumptions characterizing the positivist
view of the social sciences, it is no surprise that it has perpetuated
a fundamental disregard for the social relations of *power* in its
definitions of culture. Michel Foucault (1977) describes this
phenomenon as stemming from a "historical problem" arising
from the fact that "the West has insisted for so long on seeing
power . . . as juridical and negative rather than as technical and
positive" (p. 121). He challenges the resulting positive mechanisms
and the juridical schematism so prevalent in these characteriza-
tions of the nature of power that isolate any discussions of power
to limited social spheres and theoretically dichotomize it into instances related solely to questions of domination or powerlessness.

It is this undialectical position held by the dominant social
sciences that has failed to perceive power as both a negative and
positive force, and as a force that works both on and through people (Giroux, 1988b). One of the major services that this negation
of power has provided for the dominant culture has been a
multitude of covert avenues of control with which to determine
what is to constitute truth in a given society. Foucault (1977) sheds
light on the issue by defining truth as "the ensemble of rules according to which the true and the false are separated and specific
effects of power [are] attached to the true" (p. 132). Within this
perspective, truth is perceived in terms of a "regime of truth"
where it exists "in a circular relation with systems of power which
produce and sustain it, and to effects of power which it induces
and which extend it" (p. 133).

Hence, in order to understand the relationship between culture
and power we must also comprehend the dynamics that exist between what is considered truth (or knowledge) and power. It is
this relationship that has seldom been questioned with respect to
its effect on schooling and its control of what constitutes
knowledge in American schools. Foucault's description of the

dynamics at work in the relationship between truth and power can prove helpful in an inquiry of this nature:

Truth is a thing of this world: it is produced only by virtue of multiple forms of constraint. And it induces regular effects of power. Each society [culture] has its regime of truth, its "general politics" of truth: that is, the types of discourse which it accepts and makes function as true; the mechanisms and instances which enable one to distinguish true and false statements; the means by which each is sanctioned; the techniques and procedures accorded value in the acquisition of truth; the status of those who are charged with saying what counts as true. (Foucault, 1977, p. 131)

An implicit but important assumption drawn from Foucault's work is that, if schools are to move toward a context of cultural democracy, then it must be recognized that the ability of individuals from different cultural groups to express their cultural truths is clearly related to the power that certain groups are able to wield in the social order. Therefore, any educational theory of cultural democracy must challenge how meanings and values for "truth" are imposed and perpetuated in schools through the dialectical and social mechanisms of economic and political control found in the society at large.

A REDEFINITION OF CULTURE

In concerted efforts to unearth the fundamentally political nature of culture, Giroux (1981, 1983, 1985, 1988a, 1988b) has consistently addressed the critical connection between culture and power in his educational theories on ideology, cultural politics, and the hidden curriculum. His notion of culture incorporates the range of relationships exercised among social groups that is generally determined by the nature of social structures and material conditions and mediated, in part, by the power inherent in the dominant culture. There are two important conditions active in this definition:

The first centers around the material conditions that arise from asymmetrical relations of power and the principles emerging from different

/ *ADINERADOS*

classes and groups who use them to make sense of their location in a given society. The second condition refers to the relations between capital and its dominant classes, on the one hand, and the cultures and experiences of the subordinate classes on the other. In this relationship, capital is constantly working to produce the ideological and cultural conditions essential to maintain itself, or the social relationships needed to produce the rate of profit. (Giroux, 1983, p. 163)

From the standpoint of these two conditions, Giroux posits a notion of culture as a dialectical instance of power and conflict that results from the constant struggle over material conditions and the form and content of everyday life. The meaning and nature of culture, as such, is derived out of the lived experiences of different social groups and the practical activities of ownership, control, and maintenance of institutions. From this perspective, the structures, material practices, and lived relations of a given society are not in themselves a unified culture, but rather a complex combination of dominant and subordinate cultures that serve the function of the society itself. A phenomenon that is "forged, reproduced, and contested under conditions of power and dependency that primarily serve the dominant culture" (Giroux, 1983, p. 163).

Burgeses vs proletariado

DOMINANT AND SUBORDINATE CULTURES

A dialectical view of culture and its link to social power is essential to understanding the logic that supports the various forms of dominant and subordinate power relations that exist in American society. Inherent in this view is the notion that culture does not function in a social vacuum, but rather as a system that is characterized by social stratification and tensions (Freire & Macedo, 1987). Along these lines, Richard Johnson's (1983) perspective on culture provides an excellent starting point for conceptualizing pedagogical issues related to dominant and subordinate cultures in terms of relations of power. In his definition, he incorporates the following three principles:

Cultural + relaciones sociales

The first is that cultural processes are intimately connected with social relations, especially with class relations and class formations, with sexual

divisions, with the racial structuring of social relations, and with age oppression as a form of dependency. The second is that culture involves
power and helps to produce asymmetries in the abilities of individuals
and social groups to define and realize their needs. And the third . . . is
that culture is neither autonomous nor an externally determined field,
but a site of social differences and struggles. (Johnson, 1983, p. 11)

DEFINICIÓN: de Cultura dominante

Johnson's definition of culture provides the context for looking
at the social dynamics of subordinate cultures and how relations
of power and culture directly impact on the lives of students of
color. Generally speaking, the *dominant culture* refers to
ideologies, social practices, and structures that affirm the central
values, interests, and concerns of those who are in control of the
material and symbolic wealth in society. The *subordinate culture*
refers to groups who exist in social and material subordination
to the dominant culture (McLaren, 1988).

It is significant to note that subordinate cultures are maintained
in oppressive conditions not only through the dominant culture's
function to legitimate the interests and values of the dominant
groups, but also through an ideology that functions to marginalize
and invalidate cultural values, heritage, language, knowledge, and
lived experiences—all of which constitute essential elements for
the survival of subordinate cultures. Keeping this in mind, it is
also important to note that subordinate cultures are situated and
recreated within life processes of society that are strongly informed by relations of domination, resistance, and affirmation.

Las reacciones de los oprimidos

IDEOLOGY

The work of critical theorists at the Institute of Social Research
(Das Institute fur Sozialforschung), better known as the Frankfurt
School, reflects some of the earliest concerns about those traditional positivist definitions of culture that perceive it as autonomous and unrelated to the political and economic power
structuring the life processes of society. Theodor Adorno (1967),
a major contributor to the Frankfurt School's investigation into
the question of culture and power as it relates to the notion of
ideology, argues,

[The conventional view of culture] overlooks what is decisive: the role of ideology in social conflicts. To suppose, if only methodologically, anything like an independent logic of culture is to collaborate in the hypostasis of culture. . . . [T]he substance of culture . . . resides not in culture alone but in relation to something external, to the material life-process. Culture as Marx observed of juridical and political systems, cannot be fully *understood, either in terms of itself . . . or in terms of the so-called universal development of the mind.* To ignore this . . . is to make ideology the basic matter and to establish it firmly. (Giroux, 1983, p. 22; emphasis added)

The Frankfurt School has been instrumental in developing an analysis of culture that assigns it a key position in the development of historical experience as much as in daily life. The Frankfurt theorists conclude that the notion of culture in Western society has been redefined by repressive forms of positivist rationality. Hence, culture has been reified and the cultural realm has been appropriated as a new locus of social control under which the domination of nature and society precede technological progress and economic growth. To describe this phenomenon, Adorno coins the term *culture industry* in response to the institutionalization of culture as an industrial force that not only produces goods but also legitimates the logic of capital and its institutions through its mechanism of rationalization and standardization of dominant beliefs and values—namely, ideology (Giroux, 1983).

Mark Horkheimer (1972), a founder and major theorist of the Frankfurt School, defines ideology as an individual or set of claims, perspectives, and philosophies that function to mask or conceal the social contradictions in society on behalf of the ruling class. David Held describes the Frankfurt School's characterization of ideology as

forms of consciousness [that] claim to represent generalizable interests but conceal the particular and sectarian interests of the ruling class; and/or insofar as they maintain that, societal outcomes represent natural ones, when they are the result of particular constellations of human relations; and/or insofar as they glorify the social situation as harmonious when it is, in fact, conflict-ridden. Ideologies are not . . . merely illusions. They are embodied and manifested in social relations [transformed] into

impersonal and reified forms . . . express[ing] modes of existence. . . .
[I]deologies are often also packages of symbols, ideas, and theories
through which people experience their relation to each other and the
world. . . . [I]deologies mystify social relations or adequately reflect distorted social relations. (Held, 1980, p. 186)

An example of ideology is present in capitalist social relationships based on class interests that in practice negate individual
autonomy, despite ideological adherence to the doctrine of individualism. This can be better understood by looking at Horkheimer's analysis of capitalist production and exchange, which conditions people to work for themselves. Capitalism's individualistic
ideological underpinnings simultaneously emphasize and deny the
individual's subjectivity. On the one hand, the individual's subjectivity is emphasized because the individual, freed from the bon-
dages of feudalism, has become free to buy and sell on the open
market. The individual's material success becomes a guideline for
judging right and wrong; and consequently, this success also
becomes both the sign and reward of individual development. On
the other hand, the individual's subjectivity is denied because she
or he is isolated in the context of buying and selling. Exchange
processes become the mode in which individuality is organized and
claimed. The pursuit of self-interest is equated with the pursuit
of individual material interests. Hence, the liberal defense of individual freedom becomes ideology, for it masks the particular
interests that inform its structure (Held, 1980).

This notion of ideology is pedagogically significant in that it most
specifically relates to the ideas and practices through which consciousness (whether understood as "true" or "false") is formed
and expressed in society (Davies, 1981). Culture and ideology are
then linked through the production of all forms of consciousness,
which include ideas, feelings, desires, moral preferences, and subjectivities. In this respect, schools play a major cultural role as
sites where ideologies are produced and perpetuated in society.
It is this function of schools in the *production, interpretation, and
effectivity of meaning* that must be understood in terms of a dialectical relationship between culture and power, in order to assure
that ideology can serve as a *pedagogical tool of investigation* rather
than an instrument of domination (Giroux, 1983).

Also critical to an understanding of how ideology works on and through individuals is the Frankfurt School's notion of *depth psychology*, developed by Herbert Marcuse (1955). Influenced by Sigmund Freud's theories of the unconscious and instinct, Marcuse conceives of ideology as existing in the depth of the individual's psychological structure of needs, common sense, and critical consciousness. Thus, instead of limiting his notion of ideology only to external social processes, Marcuse dialectically defines it as forms of historically rooted domination that exist both in the socioeconomic structure of society as well as in the sedimented history or psychological structure of the individual. In this manner, he seeks to explain "that the struggle against freedom reproduce[s] . . . in the psyche of man [and woman] as the self-repression of the repressed individual, and his self-repression in turn sustains his masters and their institutions" (Marcuse, 1955, p. 16). This view of ideology can begin to assist educators to understand the function of ideology and the process of cultural hegemony that results via schooling theories and practices encased in a myriad of social contradictions and unresolved conflicts.

HEGEMONY

Antonio Gramsci (1971) was one of the first to argue that educators need to understand how the dominant culture structures ideology and produces social practices in schools, for the purpose of shattering the mystification of the existing power relationships and the social arrangements that sustain them. Gramsci's theory of *cultural hegemony* is based on the notion that the supremacy of a social group manifests itself in two ways: as *domination* and as *intellectual and moral leadership*. Through his inquiry into the nature of hegemony, Gramsci's intent is to unravel the entanglements between the forces of political power, cultural ideology, and pedagogy that result in the domination of subordinated groups. Giroux elaborates further on Gramsci's theory of hegemony:

Hegemony refers to a form of ideological control in which dominant beliefs, values, and social practices are produced and distributed throughout a whole range of institutions such as schools, the family, mass media, and trade unions. . . . The complexity of hegemonic control is an important point to stress, for it refers not only to those isolatable meanings and ideas that the dominant [culture] imposes on others, but also to those lived experiences that make up the texture and rhythm of daily life. (Giroux, 1981, p. 94)

en la industria

The theory of hegemony has emerged from a concern with the changing forms of domination that have developed in advanced industrial societies. With the rise of modern science and technology, social control has been exercised less through the use of physical deterrents and increasingly through the distribution of an elaborate system of norms and imperatives. Gramsci notes that—unlike fascist regimes, which control primarily through physically coercive forces and arbitrary rules and regulations— capitalist societies utilize forms of hegemonic control that function systematically by winning the consent of the subordinated to the authority of the dominant culture (Gramsci, 1971).

ganándose por control uniento por lo que no por la fuerza

At the heart of hegemonic control is political power—a power derived from control of the social structures and natural configurations that embody routines and practices inherent in different social relationships resulting from both the content and the manner in which knowledge is structured in society. It represents a power that is maintained through selective silence and is manifested in the fragmentation of social definitions, managements of information and the subsequent shaping of popular attention, consent, belief, and trust (Forester, 1985). Peter McLaren describes this hegemonic force as

a cultural encasement of meaning, a prison house of language and ideas, that is freely entered in both by dominators and dominated. . . . [T]he dominant culture is able to manufacture dreams and desires for both dominant and subordinate groups by supplying terms of reference (i.e., images, visions, stories, ideals) against which all individuals are expected to live their lives [and] in which the values of the dominant [culture] appear so correct that to reject them would be unnatural, a violation of common sense. (McLaren, 1988, p. 174)

En las escuelas

Hegemony in American schools results, more specifically, from institutionalized social relations of power that are systematically asymmetrical, and therefore unequally privilege students from the dominant culture over students from subordinate cultures. This institutional hegemonic process is most often achieved through four different modes of domination: legitimation, dissimulation, fragmentation, and reification (McLaren, 1988). *Legitimation* constitutes a form of domination that is perpetuated through its presentation of a particular set of power relations as legitimate and eminently just and fair. This mode of hegemonic control is clearly reflected in the manner in which educational institutions justify a system of meritocracy in American schools. *Dissimulation* describes instances where subordinate group domination is concealed, denied, or obscured. An example of dissimulation is found in school practices related to student tracking and ability grouping. *Fragmentation* is achieved through relations of domination, which are maintained primarily through the production of meaning that fragments groups and places them in opposition to one another. Fragmentation is readily apparent in faculty interpretations of student affirmative action and its negative impact on admission criteria. *Reification* results when transitory historical states of affairs are presented as permanent, natural, and commonsensical, as if they were frozen or fixed in the passage of time. The neo-conservative movement's call for a return to the Great Books is an example of this mode of domination.

Many more forms of domination are readily visible in American schools, but none is more effective than those woven tightly into the fabric of classroom curriculum. Giroux (1983), who has written extensively on the hidden curriculum, identifies several ways in which hegemony is actualized through school curriculum, including the following: (1) the selection of cultural values and materials deemed socially legitimate; (2) the categories utilized for classifying certain cultural content and forms as superior and inferior; (3) the selection and legitimation of school and classroom relationships; and (4) the distribution of and access to different types of culture and knowledge by different social classes. Through these common curricular practices, schools secure teacher participation in a variety of forms of cultural invasion and the subsequent subordination of bicultural students.

CULTURAL INVASION *a Través de las escuelas*

Throughout American institutions, the dominant culture utilizes forms of cultural hegemony to exert domination and control over people of color and, by so doing, perpetuates a condition that Freire (1970) calls *cultural invasion*. Cultural invasion represents an antidialogical action that serves in the sustained social, political, and economic oppression of subordinate groups. Freire describes cultural invasion as an act in which

Imponiendo solo su punto de vista
the invaders penetrate the cultural context of another group, in disrespect of the latter's potentialities; they impose their own view of the world upon those they invade and inhibit the creativity of the invaded by curbing their expression. . . . The invaders act; those they invade have only the illusion of acting through the action of the invaders. . . . All domination involves invasion . . . a form of economic and cultural domination. (Freire, 1970, p. 150)

Given the dynamics inherent in cultural invasion, any attempt to create effectively a critical foundation for bicultural education must also challenge those forms of ideological hegemony that result in further domination of students based on the color of their skin and the language they speak. How the dominant culture perpetuates language domination and racism and their effect on bicultural students must be examined if educators are effectively to create a context of cultural democracy in the classrooms.

Language Domination *Solo Ingles*

Language domination is sustained via a twofold process. First, the language that many bicultural students bring to the classroom is systematically silenced and stripped away through values and beliefs that support its inferiority to standard English. Second, the traditional literacy process in American schools perpetuates subordinate social relations through an instrumental approach that works to discourage the development of critical literacy among bicultural students.

Many bicultural students are forced to contend with institutional negation and disrespect of their linguistic codes. In many schools

Prohibido hablar otro idioma

bicultural students are not only discouraged but actively prevented from speaking their native languages (e.g., Spanish, Japanese, Chinese, Ebonics, etc.). Educators justify these practices with concerns that the native language will interfere with the student's intellectual and emotional development (Ramirez & Castaneda, 1974). Even where bilingual programs exist, these values and beliefs are reflected strongly in school policies that encourage the rapid mainstreaming of bicultural students into English-only environments or provide only English as a Second Language (ESL) instruction to students who are limited English speakers. Paulo Freire and Donald Macedo (1987) point to the asymmetrical power relations reflected in these attitudes:

[The] English [only] movement in the United States . . . points to a xenophobic culture that blindly negates the pluralistic nature of U.S. society and falsifies the empirical evidence in support of bilingual education, as has been amply documented. These educators, including the present Secretary of Education William Bennett, fail to understand that it is through multiple discourses that students generate meaning in their everyday social context. (Freire & Macedo, 1987, p. 154)

The hegemonic forces of class oppression and cultural invasion strongly converge in the dynamics of language domination. The set of values and power relations that inform the current neoconservative perspective on bilingualism are very similar to those of other Western European colonizers[1] who have insisted that colonized children be taught in the European language and who, by way of this process, have attempted to strip away systematically the cultural integrity and independence of the native people they wish to control and dominate. It is critical that educators recognize the role language plays as one of the most powerful transmitters of culture; as such, it is crucial to the survival of a cultural community. Within the student's native language is contained the codification of lived experiences that provide the avenues for students to express their own realities and to question the wider social order. Gramsci, in his work on cultural hegemony, identified the hidden forces that underlie the seriousness of this process: "Each time that, in one way or another, the question of language comes to the fore, that signifies that a series of other problems is about to emerge, the formation and enlarging of the ruling class, the necessity to establish more intimate and sure relations between the ruling groups and the national popular masses, that is, the reorganization of cultural hegemony" (Freire & Macedo, 1987, p. 150).

Hence, negating the native language and its potential benefits in the development of the student's voice constitutes a form of psychological violence and functions to perpetuate social control over subordinate language groups through various linguistic forms of cultural invasion. Nowhere is there a more poignant example than the history of Native American Indian children, who have been forced to leave their families and their cultural community on the reservation to attend government schools.

Language domination silences student voices and seriously curtails their active participation in school life. With few opportunities to enter into dialogue and reflect on their reality and lived experiences in terms of political and historical contexts, many bicultural students are marginalized and isolated. School practices associated with this form of hegemony ultimately hinder students' critical capacities and prevent the development of the understanding necessary to struggle effectively toward empowerment.

Racism

Racism represents one of the most violent forms of human oppression that exists in American society and yet, it seems, one of the most difficult for most individuals of the dominant culture to comprehend. Often the difficulty arises in the faulty perceptions and assumptions that persist in the deep hegemonic consciousness of most Anglo-Americans. In addition to strong ethnocentric values, much of the difficulty is related to the pervasive individualistic ideology of the dominant culture that effectively truncates the ability of most Anglo-Americans to move from an individual context to an institutional context, particularly when the issue is associated with subordination along color lines. Yet, the ability to comprehend institutionally is essential to the struggle against racism and other forms of social oppression in American schools.

Ethnocentrism is defined as a notion that one's race, nation, and culture is superior to all others (Knowles & Prewitt, 1969). It is most often manifested by the establishment of standards of behavior by which everything is judged and compared. These standards are based on the implicit assumptions of the dominant culture that holds power in a multicultural society (Phillips, 1979). Ethnocentrism is particularly prevalent in the color-blind and melting-pot views that continue to exist in American schools. The underpinnings of White supremacy at work here function to silence the voices of bicultural students by ignoring the daily lived experiences of race oppression. Further, this view supports an assimilation bias held by the majority of teachers that fails to perceive the racism inherent in consistently judging and comparing bicultural students' success to that of students from the dominant culture, and in expecting bicultural students to incorporate dominant cultural values as their own. Many teachers espouse the ethos of considering all people to be the same without acknowledging the asymmetrical relations of power in the United States nor considering that many bicultural students might, in fact, already possess cultural values essential to their survival, given their particular histories and struggles in the face of racism.

It is worth noting that the notion of a universal ranking of human beings in a hierarchical order is well integrated within all perspectives that support an ethnocentric view of the world (Hodge et al., 1975). *Social Darwinism* represents an excellent example of the ideology of cultural racism in the social sciences. Social scientists extend the evolutionary notions of a single developmental pattern and the survival of the fittest into the realm of human development. These theories of human development are then transplanted into the classroom and both negatively and deceptively influence the perceptions of teachers toward students of subordinate cultures by their efforts to emphasize the universalism of human development, while they ignore the reality of differences that exist in society.

Further, Robert Blauner (1972) argues that teachers who defend the dominant culture often depict or interpret a cultural reality that is not their own in an inauthentic manner. As such, they are very likely to miss the essence, nuances, and inner complexities of living in a bicultural world and thus invalidate the lived experiences of students of color. This is particularly the case with monocultural teachers who are limited, for the most part, to a dominant cultural view of the world. Hence, they often reject the definitions that bicultural students have of themselves and their communities and, as a consequence, violate the students' self-determination.

The inability of the dominant culture to accept the reality of people of color as legitimate is intensified by the repressed contradictions that have existed since the advent of American society. This dynamic is well documented through historical fact, which clearly reveals that, in spite of espoused principles of justice, liberty, and equality for all, subordinate cultures have suffered from blatant discrimination in this country. Blacks share a history of slavery; Puerto Ricans, Mexicans, and Filipinos share a history of colonization; Native American Indians share a history of near-extinction; Chinese share a history of exploitation for cheap labor; and Japanese share a history of retention camps. Despite the critical roles that these events have played in the historical and social development of each group, all have been, for the most part, systematically ignored or whitewashed in traditional social studies curricula and textbooks used in American schools.

The distinction between *individual racism* and *institutional racism* can best be understood in respect to the collective power than can be utilized to subordinate a group. Stokely Carmichael and Charles Hamilton, discussing racism in the Black community, give the following definition in an effort to clarify the difference: "Racism is both overt and covert. It takes two, closely related forms: individual whites acting against blacks, and acts by the total white community against the black community. We call these individual racism and institutional racism" (Knowles and Prewitt, 1969, p. 1).

Some concrete examples may help to shed some light on this distinction. When a teacher consistently harasses bicultural students because they do not speak proper English, this is an act of individual racism. But when the parents complain to the principal or school board and no action is taken by the school district to halt the teacher's actions, then it becomes a form of institutional racism. When a social studies teacher glosses over the impact of slavery on Blacks and presents the story of slaves in the South as one of benevolence, this is an act of individual racism. That this teacher is knowingly permitted by school administrators to perpetuate this racist discourse on students is an act of institutional racism.

What is most significant is that both forms of racism result from deep-rooted prejudices and stereotypes. But institutional racism is a form of racial discrimination that is woven into the fabric of the power relations, social arrangements, and practices through which collective actions result in the use of race as a criterion to determine who is rewarded in society (Knowles & Prewitt, 1969). Institutional racism can only result when it is backed by the dominant culture's institutional power to oppress. In this manner, the dynamics of institutional racism are similar to sexism[2] and classism, in that it is also institutional power that sustains the subordination of women and the working class in the United States.

Institutional forms of stereotyping constitute some of the most pervasive manifestations of racist thinking. Stereotypes of subordinate groups reflect the deep-rooted prejudices of the dominant culture that work to justify and sustain political, social, and economic inequity. Often the persistence and development of stereotypes and stereotypical caricatures can be seen historically as a cultural barometer of the racial climate, revealing quite poignantly their service to the ruling class.[3] Racial stereotypes fuel misconceptions of subordinate cultures as inferior and imprison bicultural students and their communities into hardened images that influence the manner in which they are treated in schools and in society at large.

Racial stereotypes and other racist notions have often been reflected in traditional social science and educational theory,[4] as well as other forms of institutionalized social attitudes and behaviors. What is even more disturbing is the insidious manner in which this form of cultural invasion has been perpetuated among the oppressed themselves. So often it has resulted in a process that has systematically conditioned bicultural students to identify with the assumed superiority of the dominant culture to the extent that they often participate in their oppression via an internalized inferior view of their own culture/race. Freire describes this dynamic in the following manner:

For cultural invasion to succeed, it is essential that those invaded become convinced of their intrinsic inferiority. . . . The more invasion is accentuated and those invaded are alienated from the spirit of their own culture and from themselves, the more the latter want to be like the invaders: to walk like them, dress like them, talk like them (Freire, 1970, p. 151)

It is essential for educators to recognize that, in fact—despite the extensive power of the dominant culture—seldom can forms of hegemonic power gain complete control over subordinate groups. This can best be explained through Gramsci's (1971) notion of *contradictory consciousness*. Gramsci argues that human beings view the world from a perspective that contains both hegemonic forms of thinking as well as critical insight. Thus, contradictory consciousness represents a form of common sense that is rooted in cultural folklore but at the same time is enriched with scientific ideas and philosophical opinions, which enter into ordinary daily life. From this perspective, the consciousness of subordinate cultures cannot be equated with simple passivity and one-dimensional characteristics. Instead, this consciousness has to be recognized as a complex arrangement of thought and practice that, to one degree or another, is active in the world. Consequently, it can be said that there is an ever-present consciousness of resistance that engages, consciously or unconsciously, in an ongoing struggle with the external social forces of domination and the internal human forces that seek humanization.

RESISTANCE

Whether hegemony takes place in the school, the mass media, or other social institutions, it must constantly be fought for to be maintained. It is not something that simply consists of the projection of the ideas of the dominant classes into the heads of the subordinate classes. The footing on which hegemony moves and functions has to shift ground constantly in order to accommodate the changing nature of historical circumstances and the complex demands and critical actions of human beings (Aronowitz & Giroux, 1985).

This is most apparent when oppositional ideologies of subordinate cultures attempt to resist and challenge the dominant ideologies in an effort to break through the existing relations of power. Often the dominant culture is able to manipulate alter-native and oppositional ideologies in a manner that more readily secures its hegemony. The celebrations of Cinco de Mayo and Mar-tin Luther King's birthday are prime examples of how these in-itially radical concepts—intended to resist cultural invasion—have been appropriated in such a fashion that they now do little to challenge the real basis of power of the dominant culture.

Yet, despite this hegemonic control, members of subordinate cul-tures continue to resist in an effort to struggle for power and control over their own lives. Giroux elaborates on the nature of *resistance*:

Resistance has been defined as a personal space, in which the logic and force of domination is contested by the power of subjective agency to subvert the process of socialization. Seen this way, resistance functions as a type of negation or affirmation placed before ruling discourses and practices. Of course, resistance often lacks an overt political project and frequently reflects social practices that are informal, disorganized, apolitical, and atheoretical in nature. In some instances it can reduce itself to an unreflective and defeatist refusal to acquiesce to different forms of domination, or even naive rejection of oppressive forms of moral and political regulation. (Giroux, 1988a, p. 162)

As the above suggests, resistance manifests itself in a multitude of ways. Two major categories particularly significant to the classroom are related to the way that many bicultural students may respond toward teachers, even when there is an attempt to create the conditions for cultural democracy in the classroom. In the first instance, bicultural students participate in oppositional behaviors that are centrally linked to the act of resisting the domi-nant ideological patterns of knowledge and relationships of power that are in direct conflict and contradiction with their lived ex-periences. In the second, resistance points to an act directed toward resisting any challenge to the dominant culture that would require the student to engage critically in a redefinition of the self. Here, the student of color struggles to hold onto the domi-nant culture's view of the world (as described by Freire). It is im-portant to note that, due to the contradictory nature of hegemonic control, most bicultural students exhibit these and many other forms of resistance at any given moment.

McLaren (1988) addresses the notion of resistance in students of subordinate cultures as a means of empowerment, a celebration of pleasure, and a struggle against oppression in the lived historicity of the moment: "To resist means to fight against the monitoring of passion and desire. . . . Resistance is a rejection of the reformulation as docile objects where spontaneity is replaced by efficiency, in compliance with the needs of the corporate marketplace" (p. 188).

Many forms of resistance by subordinate cultures have also been historically played out on the cultural terrain that encompasses language. Often the refusal to be literate has constituted an act of resistance rather than an act of ignorance, in that oppressed groups may have refused—consciously or unconsciously—to learn the specific cultural codes and competencies of the dominant culture, as a protective mechanism. Freire and Macedo (1987) point to the fact that language can shed light on the manner in which subordinate cultures have resisted forms of cultural invasion, and in so doing can provide a glimpse of how people survive.

This chapter has examined the relationship between culture and power as a fundamental step toward the development of a critical bicultural pedagogy of education. This discussion has begun to deconstruct those social relations of power that frame the traditional cultural discourse, to analyze the forms and nature of domination experienced by subordinate cultures, and, in addition, to search out those theories that can best shed some light on the impact of these asymmetrical power relations on the education of subordinate cultures in American society. Without a clear understanding of the effects these forces have on the nature of schooling and the lives of bicultural students, it would be impossible to move effectively toward a critical theory of cultural democracy.

NOTES

1. For a discussion concerning the effects of language domination on colonized native populations, see *The Colonizer and the Colonized* (Memmi, 1965, pp. 104–11).

2. Although women of color in the United States must indeed deal with the issue of sexism and its impact on their lives, due to the limited focus of this project it will not be dealt with directly in this book. For excellent

discussions of the issue and its relationship to education, see *Women Teaching for Change* (Weiler, 1985) and *Talking Back* (Hooks, 1989).

3. An excellent historical account on the development of Black caricature in the United States is found in the film *Ethnic Notions*, by Marlin Riggs (California Newsreel, 1987) and in *Ethnic Notions: Black Images in the White Mind*, published by Berkeley Art Center and based on Janette Faulkner's collection of artifacts that was the inspiration for the project.

4. A historical documentation of the impact of racism on social science theories is found in *The Mismeasure of Man* (Gould, 1981).

CHAPTER 3

A CRITICAL THEORY OF CULTURAL DEMOCRACY

> Education has to be linked to forms of self and social empower-
> ment if the school is to become . . . a force in the ongoing struggle
> for democracy as a way of life.
>
> Henry Giroux
> *Schooling and the Struggle for Public Life*

Through the process of examining more fully the link between
culture and power, it becomes quite evident that in order to move
toward a genuinely liberatory form of education there must exist
in theory and practice an emancipatory political construct on
which to build a critical bicultural pedagogy. This is particularly
true given the asymmetrical power relations in American society
and the disproportionate number of injustices suffered by students
of color in the public schools. Significant to this discussion is the
notion of student voice and empowerment and the conditions required for bicultural students to develop their *bicultural voice* and
experience a process of empowerment in the classroom. In more
specific terms, there must exist a democratic environment where
the lived cultures of bicultural students are critically integrated
into the pedagogical process.
  Keeping these principles in mind, a critical theory of cultural
democracy emerges as part of a language of possibility and hope.

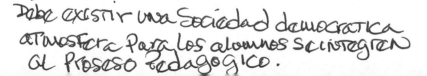

Debe existir una Sociedad democratica
atmosfera para los alumnos se integren
al proseso pedagogico.

In the same spirit of human equality and social justice that is so clearly found in John Dewey's (1916) writings on democratic schooling and, more recently, in the work of Henry Giroux (1988a) on critical democracy, a critical theory of cultural democracy seeks to function as an educational construct that can transform the nature of classroom life. Above all, it represents a concerted effort to awaken the bicultural voice of students of color and cultivate their critical participation as active social agents in this world. This is particularly essential in light of the many social forces of domination at work in the lives of bicultural students.

A philosophy of *cultural democracy* was defined originally by Mexican-American educators Manuel Ramirez and Alfredo Castaneda (1974). It is based primarily on the principle that every individual has the right to maintain a *bicultural identity*. Since the critical theory of cultural democracy to be developed in this chapter is an effort to expand on some of the ideas formulated in the original theory, the meaning of biculturalism and its implications for establishing a culturally democratic environment must first be considered as a necessary part of a culturally emancipatory discourse.

BICULTURALISM

Biculturalism refers to a process wherein individuals learn to function in two distinct sociocultural environments: their primary culture, and that of the dominant mainstream culture of the society in which they live. It represents the process by which bicultural human beings mediate between the dominant discourse of educational institutions and the realities that they must face as members of subordinate cultures. More specifically, the *process of biculturation* incorporates the different ways in which bicultural human beings respond to cultural conflicts and the daily struggle with racism and other forms of cultural invasion.

It is essential that educators recognize that, just as racism constitutes a concrete form of domination directly experienced only by people of color, biculturalism specifically addresses the different strategies of survival adopted by people of color in response to the dynamics of living in constant tension between conflicting

cultural values and conditions of cultural subordination. Although
the responses may bear a similarity to those that result from conditions of class oppression, an analysis of biculturalism cannot be
reduced simply to notions of class conflict. The "attack on culture
is more than a matter of economic factors. [I]t differs from the
class situation of capitalism precisely in the importance of culture
as an instrument of domination" (Blauner, 1972, p. 67). Thus,
simply to consider the lived experiences of bicultural populations
as only dictated by forces related to class conflict is to fall into
a reductionistic theoretical trap that results in trivializing and
distorting the cultural struggles for equality of people of color in
the United States.

In examining the notion of biculturalism, it is of major significance that, since the early 1900s, writers, educators, and social
theorists of color have made references in their work to the
presence of some form of dual or separate socialization process
among their own people. These references have included a variety of constructs used to describe the personality development,
identity, or traits of non-Whites socialized in a racist society: double consciousness (DuBois, 1903); double vision (Wright, 1953);
bicultural (Valentine, 1971; deAnda, 1984; Ramirez & Castaneda,
1974; Red Horse et al., 1981; Solis, 1980; Rashid, 1981); diunital
(Dixon & Foster, 1971); multidimensional (Cross, 1978); and other
references that closely resemble notions of duality and twoness
(Memmi, 1965; Fanon, 1967; Kitano, 1969; Hsu, 1971; Sue & Sue,
1978).

These many studies of Black, Latino, Asian, and Native American populations clearly indicate that a bicultural phenomenon is
present in the development of people of color. They also support
the notion of biculturalism as a mechanism of survival that constitutes forms of adaptive alternatives in the face of hegemonic
control and institutional oppression. Further, these alternatives
must be understood as forms of resistance that may—or may
not—function in the emancipatory interest of the individuals who
utilize them in their lives. In order to understand better the role
of biculturalism in relation to a theory of cultural democracy, it
is helpful to examine some of these studies more closely.

Charles Valentine (1971) was one of the first social theorists to
consider the concept of a *bicultural model of human development*,

based on his work with Black children. His work represents an early attempt to expand on the *cultural difference model* and to challenge directly and displace the *cultural deprivation model*, which has failed to portray with accuracy the socialization process of children of color in the United States. Valentine suggests that bicultural groups undergo a dual socialization process that consists primarily of enculturation experiences within one's culture of origin (subordinate culture), in addition to less comprehensive but significant exposure to the socialization forces within the dominant culture. In reference to this notion of development, he writes,

The idea of biculturation helps explain how people learn and practice both mainstream culture and ethnic culture at the same time. Much intra-group socialization is conditioned by ethnically distinct experience, ranging from linguistic and other expressive patterns through exclusive associations like social clubs and recreational establishments to the relatively few commercial products and mass media productions designed for ethnic markets. Yet at the same time, members of all [subordinate cultures] are thoroughly enculturated in dominant culture patterns by mainstream institutions, including most of the contents of the mass media, most products and advertising for mass marketing, the entire experience of public schooling, constant exposure to national fashion, holidays, and heroes. (Valentine, 1971, p. 143)

Diane deAnda's (1984) efforts to examine the bicultural process and to explain the differences found among bicultural individuals has led her to suggest six factors that she argues have an influence on the level of biculturalism in the individual. These factors include the following:

1. the degree of overlap or commonality between the two cultures with regard to norms, values, beliefs, perceptions, and the like;
2. the availability of cultural translators, mediators, and models;
3. the amount and type (positive and negative) of corrective feedback provided by each culture regarding attempts to produce normative behaviors;
4. the conceptual style and problem-solving approach of the bicultural individual and their mesh with the prevalent or valued styles of the majority culture;

5. the individual's degree of bilingualism; and

6. the degree of dissimilarity in physical appearance from the majority culture, such as skin color, facial features, and so forth.

The major conceptual difference between Valentine's and deAnda's models of biculturalism lies in the manner in which the individual is considered to interrelate with the two distinct cultures. Whereas Valentine's model of biculturalism perceives the process as resulting from the bicultural individual stepping in and out of two separate and distinct cultures, deAnda's argues that the bicultural experience is possible only because an overlap exists between the two cultures. The more overlap there is between the two cultures, the more effective the bicultural process of dual socialization.

The bicultural world of Mexican-American children is described by Ramirez and Castaneda (1974) as encompassing the realities that Mexican-American children must learn in order to function effectively in the mainstream of the American cultural community, and to continue to function effectively in and contribute to the Mexican-American cultural community. They characterize this phenomenon as follows:

Los niños Mex-Am-tienen que aprende para encajar en esta sociedad

If a Mexican-American child has been raised during his [or her] preschool years in the sociocultural system characteristic of the traditional Mexican-American community, the socialization practices pertaining to (1) language and heritage, (2) cultural values, and (3) teaching [and cognitive] styles will be unique to that system, and the child will have developed a communication, learning, and motivational style which is appropriate to it. At the same time the child begins his experience in the public schools he is required to relate to a sociocultural system whose socialization practices pertaining to language and heritage, cultural values, and teaching [and cognitive] styles are different from those experienced during his preschool years. In effect, it is a new cultural world which he must come to explore and understand. At the same time, he must continue to explore, understand, and learn to function in the heretofore familiar sociocultural system . . . represented in his home and community. These demands placed on many Mexican-American children in one sense constitute the reality of a bicultural world. (Ramirez & Castaneda, 1974, p. 29)

2 tipos de comportamien en casa en la escuela

In addition, Ramirez and Castaneda posit a summary of characteristics for what they term *traditional, dualistic, and atraditional communities*. The schematic presentation for their framework incorporates the categories of general community characteristics; the degree of identification with the family, community, and ethnic group; the definitions of status and roles; the religious ideology espoused; and the preferred cognitive mode. Individuals from *traditional* communities hold a strong Mexican worldview, speak Spanish as their primary language, have a field-sensitive cognitive style, espouse a strongly Catholic ideology, and tend to live in relative isolation from the mainstream culture. Those individuals who are said to be *dualistic* incorporate cultural values from both the Mexican and Anglo-American cultures, are bilingual, Catholic, have mixed cognitive styles, and live in more ethnically heterogeneous communities. *Atraditional* individuals maintain an Anglo-American orientation, speak English exclusively, are field independent, Protestant, and live in communities that are predominantly Anglo-American. In addition, Ramirez and Castaneda attribute the diversity observed in Mexican-American communities to these seven variables:

1. distance from the Mexican border;
2. length of residence in the United States;
3. identification with Mexican, Mexican-American, or Spanish-American history;
4. degree of American urbanization;
5. degree of economic and political strength of Mexican-Americans in the community;
6. degree of prejudice; and
7. degree of contact with non–Mexican-Americans.

Ramirez and Castaneda also view the notion of bicognitive functioning as a most important goal in the development of bicultural human beings. This not only relates to the issue of cognitive flexibility, but also to the fact that functioning effectively in two cognitive styles allows bicultural students to participate more fully in both their culture and the mainstream American culture, which can then help them to achieve a strong bicultural identity. Consequently, the concept of *bicognitive development* is a vital component of the Ramirez and Castaneda methodology, which evaluates both teachers and students in terms of field-sensitive and field-dependent cognitive styles. This assessment is primarily conducted with instruments that measure preferential modes in terms of cultural values, relational styles, incentive motivation, and other behavioral and attitudinal criteria.[1]

Based on his work with Black children, Hakim Rashid (1981) defines biculturalism as "the ability to function effectively and productively within the context of America's core institutions while simultaneously retaining [an] ethnic identity" (p. 55). He strongly argues that biculturalism is an essential developmental process if children of subordinate cultures are to develop the ability to cope with the racism and classism that permeate American society. Related to this view, Rashid posits the notion that

biculturalism should also be considered an important component of the cognitive and behavioral repertoire of all American children, for it is only through recognition of the need for biculturalism that a foundation for true multiculturalism [in society] can be built. When children have developed the ability to survive and thrive within the context of their own culture as well as that of the broader society, a genuine appreciation for the variety of cultures that comprise America is the next step. (Rashid, 1981, p. 61)

A *theory of biculturality* is described by Arnoldo Solis (1980), based on his work with Chicano populations. He defines "biculturality" (biculturalism) in an individual as the result of existing in and adapting to two cultures having substantial dissimiliarity. Solis argues that the more similar the cultures, the lesser the degree of biculturality; and on the other hand, the more the dissimilarity between the two cultures, the greater the degree of biculturality.

For Solis, the dynamics of biculturation are considered to begin when the dominant culture exerts increasing influence on the subordinate culture to accommodate and assimilate to the dominant culture's value, language, and cognitive style. At this point, a dynamic of resistance is said to develop, which causes the individual to experience cultural crisis. Within this construct, the process of biculturation is viewed as an attempt to reeastablish the intrapsychic harmony of the primary culture that is threatened by the tensions arising as a result of pressure by the dominant culture to renounce subordinate cultural values. The resolution of the *bicultural crisis* is brought about through a series of developmental stages whereby the individual becomes increasingly able to recognize the value of and is able to utilize adaptive functions from both cultures in a harmonious manner (Solis, 1981).

Although there exist some differences in the manner in which these bicultural theorists have conceptualized the notion of biculturalism, it is nonetheless evident from this discussion that an understanding of what constitutes the dynamics of biculturalism is essential to any model of education that is designed to meet the needs of students of color. This is particularly true since what has often been missing (although often mentioned) from many theories of bicultural education is a serious confrontation of the power relations that shape the nature of how bicultural students respond to the tension of cultural conflicts and the pressure to assimilate so highly prevalent in traditional American schools. Hence, a notion of biculturalism must not be reduced to an absolute determined moment or a linear developmental stage. On the contrary, its critical dimension must be emphasized through its representation of bicultural existence as a complex process encompassing all the conscious and unconscious contradictory, oppressive, and emancipatory responses that can be found along a continuum that moves, conceptually, between the primary culture and the dominant culture (see Figure 3.1). Educators who possess this dialectical understanding of biculturalism will be better equipped to assist their students of color in critically examining their lived experiences in an effort to reveal genuinely the impact that cultural domination has on their lives.

Further, given the nature of cultural domination and resistance, the process of biculturation can also be understood as patterns of responses that are shaped by the manner in which bicultural students react, adjust, and accommodate to the emotional anxiety and physical stress that result from a constant cultural dissonance. These response patterns can be perceived in a more critical manner when understood in terms of an axis relationship between culture and power that, on one hand, moves between the dominant and subordinate cultures and, on the other hand, moves between the forces of dominance and resistance (see Figure 3.2).

Figure 3.1
The Biculturation Process Represented along a Dialectical Continuum

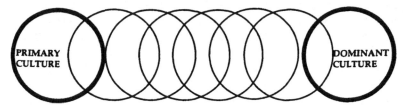

Figure 3.2
Axis Relationship between Culture and Power

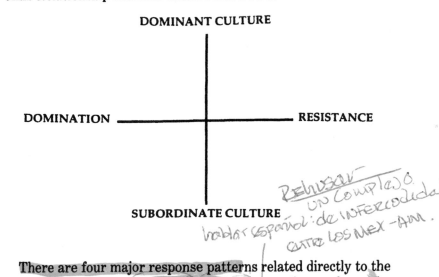

DOMINANT CULTURE

DOMINATION ——————————— RESISTANCE

SUBORDINATE CULTURE

REHUSAU un complejo de intercodidad hablar español entre los Mex-Am.

    There are four major response patterns related directly to the
biculturation process: alienation, dualism, separatism, and negotiation. Responses categorized under *cultural alienation* reflect those
that suggest an internalized identification with the dominant
culture and a rejection of the primary culture. Some examples of
alienation responses include a bicultural student's preference for
identifying herself/himself as American, refusal to speak Spanish,
belief in the inferiority of the primary culture, and denial of the
existence of racism. A *cultural dualist* (or nonnegotiation)
response pattern is informed by a perception of having two

2 culturas

separate identities: one that is identified with the primary cultural
community, and one that is related to acceptance of mainstream
institutional values. An example of a dualist response is found
among members of an all-Black social club who espouse the dominant culture's elitist bourgeois ideology. The *cultural separatist*
response pattern identifies those responses related to remaining
strictly within the boundaries of the primary culture while rejec-
ting adamantly the dominant culture. A cultural nationalist
group's responses geared toward complete self-sufficiency for its
members outside of the dominant culture represent an example
of this mode. The *cultural negotiation* response pattern reflects
attempts to mediate, reconcile, and integrate the reality of lived
experiences in an effort to retain the primary cultural identity
and orientation while functioning toward social transformation
within the society at large. Examples of cultural negotiation are
present in community struggles for bilingual education programs
in schools. It must be stressed that these patterns lie within a
social domain that can be conceptualized as a *sphere of biculturalism* (see Figure 3.3).

As such, these four patterns reflect modes of engagement that
are directly influenced by the power relations that result from
the axis relationship between power and culture. Within this
sphere of biculturalism, student responses can also be considered
with respect to the degree that they support a context of *bicultural
affirmation*. For example, cultural alienation and cultural
separatism responses move the individual away from bicultural
affirmation responses. In this sense, alienation responses tend to
move the bicultural student more exclusively toward the context
of the dominant culture while cultural separatism responses tend
to move the student more exclusively toward the primary (subordinate) cultural context. On the other hand, cultural dualism and
cultural negotiation responses, which result from some effort to
contend with the reality of both the dominant and subordinate
cultural realities, are more likely to result in moving the student
toward bicultural affirmation. However, it is critical that educators
remain cognizant of the fact that the forces of hegemony are constantly at work in shaping the realities that constitute the
bicultural existence. Hence, just as with other response modes,
bicultural affirmation responses may or may not necessarily result

Figure 3.3
Sphere of Biculturalism

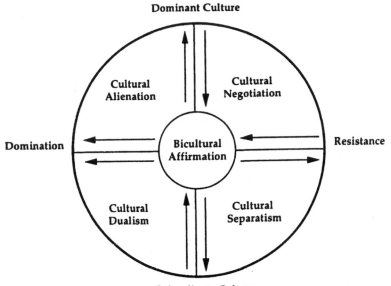

in supporting the emancipatory interests of bicultural students. Nonetheless, it is safe to say that bicultural affirmation response patterns may hold the greatest emancipatory possibility in respect to the struggle for cultural democracy in the schools.

Also vital to an understanding of biculturalism is a recognition of the relationship that exists between cultural response patterns, modes of engagement (thinking), and cultural identity (see Figure 3.4). Here again, it is helpful to utilize the four previously discussed response patterns to illustrate the dynamics inherent in the relationship between these three variables. In addition, the variable of cultural identity is presented with respect to both an individual and a social sub-category.

Cultural alienation and separatist responses are commonly reflective of a mode of engagement associated with absolute thinking,[2] which generally seeks to negate, eliminate, or move away from the tension, conflict, and contradictions that result

Figure 3.4
Relationship of Cultural Response Pattern, Mode of Engagement, and Cultural Identity

Cultural Response Pattern	Mode of Engagement	Cultural Identity	
		Individual	Social
Alienation	Absolute	Dominant	Dominant
Dualism	Dichotomized	Primary	Dominant
Separatism	Absolute	Primary	Primary
Negotiation	Critical	Primary	Bicultural

from cultural differences. This mode of engagement reinforces a form of cultural identity that is also absolute or total in nature. Hence, an alienation response pattern is commonly associated with individuals who espouse exclusively an identification with the dominant culture, while cultural separatism response patterns are associated with individuals who hold an exclusively primary cultural identity. A dichotomized mode of engagement generally results in dualism response patterns, which are likely to result from a cultural identity that is also dichotomized between the primary culture and the dominant culture. It is important to note that, although the dualist context acknowledges the existence of both cultures, its dichotomized mode of engagement also results in undialectical responses due to its efforts to avoid or deny the tension and contradictions that result from cultural conflicts. Cultural negotiation response patterns most commonly result from a critical mode of engagement that seeks to contend with the tension and contradictions inherent in cultural differences and conflicts. This dynamic functions to affirm a bicultural social identity, while reinforcing a solid individual identification with the primary culture.

Although these categories can assist educators to understand better the dynamics of the biculturation process, it is critical to remember that these patterns are not fixed. Given the contradictory nature of human consciousness and the complexity of the survival mechanisms that motivate these response patterns, bicultural students will exhibit many different variations of responses, depending on the level of their primary cultural socialization, the degree of their bilingualism, their consistent association with other bicultural students, the teacher's cultural orientation, the degree of peer pressure, institutional constraints, and other socioeconomic variables.

It is readily apparent that some of the response patterns described above incorporate principles set forth by the various bicultural theories discussed previously. But what the critical bicultural perspective proposed here attempts to do is to challenge the reductionistic and deterministic influences that shape the earlier theories of biculturalism. If educators are to meet the pedagogical needs of bicultural students, it is essential for them to recognize the ideological underpinnings that shape bicultural responses and the contradictions and tensions that result from students' efforts to survive in the midst of serious forms of educational oppression.

It is important that educators recognize that, whether or not a student from a subordinate culture perceives herself or himself as a *bicultural being*, the fact that the individual is raised within the sociocultural and class constraints dictated by the dominant culture places the student, from a sociopolitical standpoint, in a culturally subordinate position. It is the pervasive quality of hegemonic control that so often obscures the truth of this reality, particularly for those bicultural individuals who perceive themselves as adjusting successfully to the social constraints through their identification with the culture of the oppressor (Freire, 1970). This clearly points to the need for educators to examine critically bicultural responses in terms of resistance, particularly when these responses fail to result in behaviors, attitudes, or relationships that empower bicultural students by preparing them to engage as subjects in their world.

As a consequence of traditional pedagogical theories and practices, bicultural students often face isolation, alienation, and despair in public schools, because there exist few opportunities for these students to reflect together on their lived experiences and to explore critically how these experiences relate to their participation in the larger society and to their process of emancipation. Instead, student voices are silenced as "the discourse of the other" is systematically ignored in the process of schooling (Giroux, 1988a). If the bicultural voice is to be awakened and students of color are to become active social agents in the world, educators must create the conditions for a genuine form of cultural democracy to take root in the classroom.

A PHILOSOPHY OF CULTURAL DEMOCRACY

In an effort to develop a critical theory of cultural democracy, it is useful to examine first Ramirez and Castaneda's (1974) philosophy of cultural democracy for the bilingual classroom. One of the primary objectives of their work is to challenge the negative effects of the Anglo conformity/assimilation ideology of the melting pot theory, which—by implication—reduces all other cultural forms to one of inferior value, status, and importance. Hence, their notion of cultural democracy argues that

an individual can be bicultural and still be loyal to American ideals. Cultural democracy is a philosophical precept which recognizes that the way a person communicates, relates to others, seeks support and recognition from his [sic] environment . . . and thinks and learns. [Cognition] is a product of the value system of the home and community. Furthermore, educational environments or policies that do not recognize the individual's right, as guaranteed by the Civil Rights Act of 1964, to remain identified with the culture and language of his cultural group, are culturally undemocratic. (Ramirez & Castaneda, 1974, p. 23)

More specifically, the philosophy of cultural democracy argues for the right of each individual to be educated in her or his own language and learning style, which, according to Ramirez and

[handwritten: Yadopter la Comunicación]

[handwritten: El alumno Tiéne el derecho de adoptar su identidad]

Castaneda, has been found to be associated with one's language community. This also implies that every child has the right to maintain a bicultural identity—that is, the right to retain an identification with her or his culture of origin while simultaneously adopting American values and lifestyle. This philosophy encourages institutions to develop learning milieus, curriculum materials, and teaching strategies that are sensitive to the child's cultural orientation, and thus language and cognitive styles (Hernandez, 1976).

Further, the education of bicultural students within the context of a culturally democratic environment is considered by Valverde (1978) to support five specific purposes for students and the school:

1. reducing language and educational disabilities through the opportunity to learn in one's native language;
2. reinforcing the relations of the school and the home through a common bond;
3. projecting the individual into an atmosphere of personal identification;
4. giving the student a base for success in the field of work;
5. preserving and enriching the cultural and human resources of a people.

In contrast to the exclusionist Anglo conformity view, Ramirez and Castaneda characterize the culturally democratic environment as one that

[handwritten: otro Punto: de Filosofía]

1. considers the student's language, heritage, cultural values, and learning styles as educationally important;
2. views the home culture as determining unique communication, relational, incentive motivational, and cognitive styles and utilizes these styles as a basis for teacher training;
3. recognizes the child's personality as acceptable and as a means whereby the child can explore new cultural forms related to communication, human relations, incentive motivation, and cognition;
4. works to change the educational style of the school through greater parent participation, new teaching strategies, curriculum development, and assessment of techniques; and
5. holds as one of its major goals the child's formation of a bicultural identity.

Despite the many contributions of the Ramirez and Castaneda philosophy of cultural democracy to the field of bicultural education and its promise as a politicizing educational construct, it nonetheless lacks many of the critical qualities essential to the education of bicultural students as members of a subordinate culture. The deficits of the model are most apparent in the fact that it can too easily deteriorate into a positivist instrumentalist modality that perceives culture as predictable, deterministic, neutral, oversimplified, and at moments even relativistic in nature. And although it argues for changing the cultural realities of classrooms, it fails to address critically the necessary shift in power relationships required in schools and society in order to involve bicultural students in an active process of empowerment, assist them in finding their voice, and support the development of a spirit of social solidarity.

CRITICAL DEMOCRACY AND THE PROCESS OF SCHOOLING

In an effort to expand on the emancipatory intent of Ramirez and Castaneda's philosophy of cultural democracy, it would be helpful to examine the concept of *critical democracy*, particularly as it relates to the process of schooling. This would provide the critical dimension that is missing in the work of Ramirez and Castaneda and would be useful in specifically addressing the relationship of democracy to the notions of student participation and solidarity, as well as the development of voice in the process of schooling.

The term "democracy" is derived from the Greek words *demos* and *kratos*, meaning rule by the people or the many; in addition, because there were so many poor in Greece, it was taken to mean rule by the poor. Hence, despite the fact that democracy seldom has been equated with overt social conflict, historically it has never been realized without a struggle, and that struggle has always been related to social and economic equality (Arblaster, 1987). Even today, the American struggle for democracy and equality, particularly in the classroom, continues to be reflected along the lines of social class and cultural struggle.

The recognition of democracy as a site of struggle is significant to the issue of cultural democracy, where the struggle is focused specifically on the issue of culture and power and on who controls cultural truths. Unfortunately, democracy often has been reduced simplistically to an unqualified principle of majority rule, while minority groups are ignored as a part of the society at large. When this occurs—and consequently minority interests, views, and convictions are disregarded in the institutional process of decision-making, and certain groups are permanently relegated to a minority position—such a democracy is likely to become unstable and lose legitimacy in the eyes of its citizens. This results because democracy cannot function where there does not exist a sense of common will or common interest, and this cannot develop where a foundation of social and economic equality is missing. Arblaster addresses this need more specifically in his writings on democracy:

[Democracy] needs a foundation not only of shared values but also of shared experience, so that people identify with the political system to which they belong, and can trust its procedures and outcomes. This means not only that those procedures are seen and felt to be fair. It is also necessary that no significant minorities feel themselves to be permanently excluded from power and influence; that groups and individuals sense that they are roughly equal in their ability to influence the outcome of communal policymaking; and that those outcomes embody what people recognize to be the general interests of society rather than merely the combination or balance of the interests of various particular and organized groups or specific interest. (Arblaster, 1987, p. 78)[3]

From this perspective, it can be better understood why the gross and excessive forms of inequality that exist in the process of American schooling threaten the coherence of society and hence negate the principles of equality, of which democracy is an expression. It also clearly supports the notion that the contradiction between an espoused theory of democracy and a lived experience of inequality (and the obvious diffusion of power that results) is greatly responsible for the growing social tensions existing in the relationship between subordinate cultural groups and the public schools, whose pedagogical aim centers around the perpetuation of cultural domination and technocratic control. And as a further consequence, it is precisely this form of social disequilibrium that also functions effectively to prevent the concrete development of a genuine common interest and a spirit of solidarity among different groups in society. John Dewey, in writing about democratic schooling, addresses the impact that this form of inequality has on students:

In order to have a large number of values in common, all members of the group must have an equitable opportunity to receive and to take from others. There must be a large variety of shared undertakings and experiences. Otherwise, the influences which educate some into masters educate others into slaves. And the experience of each party loses in meaning when the free interchange of varying modes of life experience is arrested. . . . [This] lack of free equitable intercourse which springs from a variety of shared interests makes intellectual stimulation unbalanced. . . . The more activity is restricted to a few definite lines—as it is when there are rigid class [cultural] lines preventing adequate interplay of experiences—the more action tends to become routine on the part of the class at a disadvantage, and capricious, aimless, and explosive on the part of the class having the materially fortunate position. (Dewey, 1916, pp. 84–85)

Dewey also argues strongly that schooling in the United States should function as a primary vehicle for students to develop an ethical foundation for their participation in the process of democracy and a critical understanding of democracy as a moral ideal from which to establish a sense of community and struggle for such principles as freedom, liberty, and common good. But in order for schools to meet this challenge, Dewey proposes that educators create environments where there is a clear recognition of mutual interest as the basic factor in social control, and where there is a commitment to enter into a continuous form of readjustment through meeting the new situations produced by a variety of social discourses. He believes this to be an essential step in deconstructing the "fear of intercourse with others" by permitting conflict between students to occur so as to enable them to learn from each other and thereby expand their understanding of the world. In this context, Dewey defines democracy as

primarily a mode of associated living, of conjoint communicated experience. The extension in space of the numbers of individuals who participate in an interest so that each has to refer [her or] his own action to that of others and to consider the action of others to give point and direction to his own is equivalent to the breaking down of those barriers of class, race, and national territory which kept men [and women] from perceiving the full import of their activity. These more numerous and more varied points of contact denote a greater diversity of stimuli to which an individual has to respond; they consequently put a premium on variation in his action. They secure a liberation of powers which remain suppressed as long as the invitations to action are partial, as they must be in a group which in its exclusiveness shuts out many interests. (Dewey, 1916, p. 87)

This notion of schools as apprenticeships in democracy is also shared by Freire (1978). In his work, Freire points to the "habit of submission" that curtails subordinate classes from seeking to integrate themselves with reality, which, he argues, results from their undeveloped capacity for critical thought—a phenomenon of socially conditioned dependency and a lack of experience with participation in the democratic process. He argues that it is only through participation in an educational climate in which open dialogue is fostered that students can develop the skills for critical engagement with their world and a genuine sense of participation in a common life. Thus, Freire posits this axiom: Without dialogue, self-government cannot exist. Here, he speaks to the notion of the free and creative consciousness that results from dialogue indispensable to authentically democratic environments. He elaborates on the relationship of democracy and this idea of "transitive consciousness":

Democracy requires dialogue, participation, political and social responsibility, as well as a degree of social and political solidarity. . . . Before it becomes a political form, democracy is a form of life, characterized above all by a strong component of transitive consciousness. Such transitivity can neither appear nor develop except as men [and women] are launched into debate, participating in the examination of common problems. (Freire, 1978, pp. 28–29)

From this discussion it also becomes evident that a student's ability to participate and enter into dialogue within the classroom and, as a result, participate in a democratic social process in the world is also critically connected to the development of *voice*—that is, voice as it relates to the variety of ways by which students actively participate in dialogue and attempt to make themselves heard and understood, as well as the manner in which they define themselves as social beings. Giroux describes this concept of student voice in the following manner:

Voice refers to the principles of dialogue as they are enunciated and enacted within particular social settings. The concept of voice represents the unique instances of self-expression through which students affirm their own class, culture, racial, and gender identities. A student's voice is necessarily shaped by personal history and distinctive lived engagement with the surrounding culture. The category of voice, then, refers to the means at our disposal—the discourses available to use—to make ourselves understood and listened to, and to define ourselves as active participants in the world. . . . The concept of voice . . . provides an important basis for constructing and demonstrating the fundamental imperatives of a critical democracy. (Giroux, 1988a, p. 199)

The notion of student voice is fundamental to the struggle for democracy and equality in the classroom, particularly as it relates to the development of voice in students of color. It is connected to the control of power and the legitimation of specific student discourses as acceptable truths or rejected fallacies, and consequently determines who speaks and who is silenced. Also significant to this discussion is the reality that, when bicultural students are consistently silenced by teachers, they often are trapped in classrooms with teachers who not only prevent them from finding their voice, but who also thwart their contextual understanding of how what they are learning in the classroom can be used to transform their lives. As a result, they are conditioned into a state of dependency on a system that they do not understand and are unable to influence because they lack the critical skills necessary to participate and the social and self empowerment to make their needs, interests, and concerns heard. This, then, leads to a form of social isolation that prevents the development of a sense of community and solidarity, and that negates any possibility for a genuine process of democracy to take place in society.

Para el maestro: Estrategias

Giroux, greatly concerned with the question of voice, speaks to the kind of environment teachers must cultivate in the classroom to prevent the silencing of students:

Creación de una atmosfera en el salón

Organize classroom relationships so that students can draw on and confirm those dimensions of their own histories and experiences that are deeply rooted in the surrounding community, . . . assume pedagogical responsibility for attempting to understand the relationships and forces that influence students outside the immediate context of the classroom, . . . develop curricula and pedagogical practices around those community traditions, histories, and forms of knowledge that are often ignored within the dominant school culture, . . . create the conditions where students come together to speak, to engage in dialogue, to share their stories, and to struggle together within social relations that strengthen rather than weaken possibilities for active citizenship [and democracy]. (Giroux, 1988a, pp. 199–201)

What emerges from this discussion on democracy and the process of schooling are the fundamental principles on which to develop further a critical theory of cultural democracy. Central to any theory that seeks to speak to the notion of democracy in the classroom is the necessary requirement that it address seriously the themes of student participation, solidarity, common interest, and the development of voice. It is not enough to focus on specific cultural and/or cognitive determinants or questions related to curricular content. This is not to say that certain aspects of these educational concerns are not vital to a bicultural pedagogy, but rather to emphasize that these alone will not necessarily ensure a democratic environment. If bicultural students are to become competent in the democratic process, they must be given the opportunities to experience it actively as it gradually becomes a part of their personal history. But this can only be accomplished if there exists a culturally democratic educational environment in which students may participate actively and freely, and where they will receive the consistent support and encouragement required for them to develop their bicultural voice so they may learn to use it toward their social empowerment and emancipation.

THE AWAKENING OF THE BICULTURAL VOICE

The concept of voice constitutes one of the most important democratic essentials related to the process of student empowerment and the ability to participate in and influence the manner in which power is relegated in society—so much so that any theory of cultural democracy must specifically consider the development of voice as it relates to the pedagogical needs of bicultural students. This is particularly significant given the forces of hegemony and cultural invasion at work in the manner that bicultural students perceive themselves, their communities, and their ability to participate in the world.

As suggested in the previous section, students can only develop their voice through opportunities to enter into dialogue and engage in a critical process of reflection from which they can share their thoughts, ideas, and lived experiences with others in an open and free manner. Herein lies a primary requirement that so often is missing in the classroom experience of bicultural students. This generally occurs because the dominant pedagogy of American schools predominantly reflects the values, worldview, and belief system of the dominant culture's middle and upper classes, while it neglects and ignores the lived experiences of subordinate cultures. Hence, students of color are silenced and their bicultural experiences negated and ignored, while they are systematically educated into the discourse of the dominant culture—an ethnocentric ideology that perceives the discourse of the other as inferior, invaluable, and deficient in regard to the aims of American society. This manifests itself in various forms of cultural invasion that, consciously or unconsciously, teach bicultural students to deny their lived cultures and their bicultural voice, and to take on uncritically the ideology of the dominant culture.

In light of the hegemonic forces active in the hidden curriculum and in classroom relations, the bicultural voice can seldom develop within the school context unless students of color receive the opportunity to enter into dialogue with one another. It is primarily through the dynamics of the *bicultural dialogue* that students can come together to reflect on the common lived experiences of their bicultural process and their common responses to issues of cultural resistance, alienation, negotiation, affirmation, and oppression. In this way, bicultural students can begin to break through the rigidly held perspectives that can result when those who hold power inauthentically name their experience for them. Also important to this process is the role of the bicultural educator who functions as guide, model, and support, and who facilitates the critical (and often fearful) journey into the previously prohibited terrain of the bicultural discourse—a discourse that is often only felt or sensed, and seldom articulated. In spite of this pedagogical need, most teachers of color repeat the educational patterns they experienced as children and later learned in teacher education programs. Hence, what generally occurs in most classrooms is the silencing of the bicultural experience by teachers who have been trained to concentrate their efforts on creating an inauthentic climate of cohesion, conformity, and harmony. In so doing, they fail to involve bicultural students in their own learning and to provide opportunities for them to enter into dialogue regarding the cultural conflicts and social contradictions they experience in the classroom and in their communities.

It is precisely in meeting the student's need to participate in bicultural dialogue with others that the bicultural teacher can most provide assistance in facilitating the process across this terrain of struggle, and thus cultivate through a critical process with students a spirit of possibility and empowerment. Bicultural educators who have found their own voice can provide an effective *bicultural mirror*, which may validate, support, and encourage students through this process during moments of cognitive disequilibrium, and help them discover a language that accurately describes the feelings, ideas, and observations that previously have not fit into any of the definitions of experience provided by the dominant educational discourse. Above all, this represents a critical effort to assist students in integrating themselves as complete human beings in the world by recognizing the truths embedded in their personal reflections and the substance of their everyday lives—in essence, to awaken the bicultural voice. The development of voice and social empowerment go hand in hand as bicultural students peel away the layers of oppression and denial, undergo a deconstruction of the conditioned definitions of who they are, and emerge with a sense of their existence as historically situated social agents who can utilize their understanding of their world and themselves to enter into dialogue with those who are culturally different.

At this point, it is imperative to note that this does not mean that the bicultural voice is the only voice bicultural students need. But it does suggest that it represents a major step toward their self-empowerment, because it is the voice most intimately linked to their personal identity. Further, it is by way of the bicultural voice that students can develop the self-empowerment required to participate in the collective public voice—a voice that must be built around a collaborative effort and commitment of the many to examine critically their collective lived experiences so that together they might discover the common good. In this manner, bicultural students can also develop the ability, confidence, and desire to acknowledge the similarities, honor the differences, ex- amine the possibilities, and struggle openly with a geniune spirit of solidarity in the context of a multicultural society.

The role of the White educator in the development of the bicul- tural voice is also significant to this discussion, in that often the White teacher is one of the few people from the dominant culture with whom bicultural students have any contact on a regular basis. Consequently, the White teacher can become for the bicultural student the primary reflection of not only the public institutions, but also the society at large. How conscious teachers are of this phenomenon, as well as the histories and stories of the bicultural communities in which bicultural students reside, is fundamental to their ability to assist students in developing their voice. White educators who are working with bicultural students must first come to acknowledge their own limitations, prejudices, and biases, and must be willing to enter into dialogue with their students in a spirit of humility and with respect for the knowledge that students bring to the classroom. Despite how well-meaning many teachers may be, often it is at this juncture of power (and con- trol) that they fail bicultural students. This commonly occurs because any genuine acknowledgment of one's limitations is closely related to letting go of the control (power) associated with knowing (or holding authority), and in the process permitting the student to teach the teacher (Freire, 1970). This process truly re- quires the teacher to share the power more equitably and, in so

Observaciones en las mayorías

doing, to empower the student through critically engaging, challenging, affirming, and incorporating into the classroom the knowledge that the bicultural student has about self and community. The emphasis here is placed on the recognition that the White critical educator has much to learn from as well as to teach bicultural students in the context of a culturally democratic classroom. From students, teachers can discover what bicultural people feel, think, dream, and live, while the teachers can provide for their students the opportunity to develop their critical thinking skills, examine their histories, reflect on the world, and engage with the dominant educational discourse as free social agents who are able to influence and transform their world.

Most important to any educational theory of cultural democracy is a recognition by the educator—regardless of her or his class, race, or ethnic identity—of the emancipatory needs of students of color. In order for bicultural students to develop critical skills in the classroom, there must first exist a culturally democratic environment where bicultural students can find the opportunities to participate freely with others as they learn the forms of knowledge, values, and social practices necessary to understand how society works, where they are located in it, and what inequities exist. It is fundamental that educators remain conscious of the fact that bicultural students shape and are shaped not only by their cultural values but also by their constant struggle to survive within the myriad of cultural contradictions they face in society every day. Given this discussion, what is readily evident is the need to integrate a critical model of bicultural pedagogy built on the foundation of a cultural democracy that not only speaks to issues of particular cultural values and the development of cognitive styles, but that also critically addresses the awakening of the bicultural voice and the development of a social consciousness of struggle and solidarity that will prepare bicultural students to undertake the democratic responsibility of participation in their world, morally committed to the liberation and empowerment of all people.

NOTES

1. Ramirez and Castaneda have included in their text *Cultural Democracy: Bicognitive Development and Education* (1974) an "Appendix C:

Field-Sensitive/Field-Independent Behavioral Observation Instruments: Child and Teacher," which includes cognitive assessment tools for use in teacher and student evaluations. The primary purpose of these instruments is to assist educators in determining the degree to which a child may be bicognitive and, from the results, planning a program to increase the child's cognitive flexibility.

2. *Absolute thinking* for the purposes of this discussion is related to a view of a social reality as a totality or whole. This mode of engagement with the world is clearly sustained by the ideological tenets of identity thinking. The Frankfurt School has addressed this notion of *identity thinking* in its work related to culture. A discussion of the Frankfurt School's views on this theme can be found in "Materialism and Metaphysics," in *Critical Theory: Selected Essays* (Horkheimer, 1972); *The Dialectical Imagination* (Jay, 1973); and *Introduction to Critical Theory* (Held, 1980).

3. For an excellent investigation into the definition, historical nature, and principal ideas related to the nature of democracy, see *Democracy* by Anthony Arblaster (1987).

CHAPTER 4

CRITICAL PEDAGOGY AS A FOUNDATION FOR BICULTURAL EDUCATION

Cambiar la estructura en lugar de la buura

The solution is not to integrate them into the structure of oppression, but to transform that structure so that they can become beings for themselves.

Paulo Freire
Pedagogy of the Oppressed

Historically, bicultural education has been linked most directly to bilingual instructional theory. The powerful relationship between culture and language suggests the logic at work in this connection and the symbiotic manner in which these concepts are often discussed. As a consequence, the majority of the work in the field is most extensively focused on educational assessment, curriculum content, and teaching strategies that are related to cultural values, language, and cognition (Ramirez & Castaneda, 1974; Pialorsi, 1974; Valverde, 1978; Turner, 1982; Fishman & Keller, 1972; Ovando & Collier, 1985). Although these clearly represent primary areas of concern, the traditional manner in which these areas are addressed in the classroom does not necessarily guarantee that students will participate in a process of social empowerment, nor that they will develop their bicultural voice or become critically discursive with respect to their economic and sociopolitical reality.

A major reason for this phenomenon is the failure to change the structure of schools—a change required in order to alter the asymmetrical power relations that prevent the emancipatory development of biculturalism. Despite the extensive work directed at altering the content and language of curriculum, bicultural educators have accomplished relatively little in transforming the traditional pedagogical structure of their classrooms. As a result, bicultural students may develop a stronger sense of cultural identity, self-esteem, and both language and cognitive proficiency, while simultaneously being socialized within the context of a technocratic and instrumental pedagogy that stifles the development of critical skills and ignores questions of human agency, voice, and empowerment.

Seldom are issues of power seriously addressed with respect to the structure of classroom life. And even when educators make some effort to address the issues in their classrooms, often it is done in a "banking education" mode (Freire, 1970) that in content may be theoretically emancipatory but in practice is pedagogically oppressive. Hence, what is missing is a critical educational foundation on which bicultural educators can build a liberatory practice of bicultural education. But in order for this need to be met, teachers must struggle to change the basic structure of traditional American education.

The previous chapters have helped to illustrate the need for this structural change and to highlight the specific issues that must be considered in generating such a transformation. In addition to confronting the different forms of cultural invasion through a commitment to a culturally democratic principle, there are specific theoretical constructs related to critical pedagogy that must be incorporated in the process of establishing a critical foundation for bicultural education. UN Cambio

From the standpoint of critical theory, education must hold an emancipatory purpose and acknowledge the process of schooling as a political process. A key to this perspective is the recognition of the contextual relationship that exists between the cultural politics and economic forces in society and the structure of schools. Hence, critical pedagogy espouses a view of knowledge that is both historical and dialectical in nature. True to its critical dimensions, it is built around a serious commitment to the union of theory and practice. Further, a theory of ideology and hegemony is closely linked to critical pedagogy's concern with the nature of student resistance and its view of education as a form of counter-hegemony. And finally, critical pedagogy incorporates an understanding of critical discourse and the goal of conscientization as a consequence of the dialogical relationships that shape the structure of classroom life.

The following discussion represents an effort to outline the basic principles for a critical pedagogy that may serve effectively as a foundation for bicultural education. It is a foundation that is clearly based on an understanding of the link between culture and power and firmly rooted in a political construct of cultural democracy and a commitment to student empowerment. It represents, in theory and practice, the critical dimension that remains, for the most part, absent from the foundational groundwork of bicultural education programs in this country.

CRITICAL EDUCATION THEORY

The theoretical foundation of any educational practice must be understood by educators in order to develop fully the ability to evaluate their practice, confront the contradictions, and transform their classrooms into democratic environments where they can genuinely address the actual needs of their students—needs that result from an engagement with the real world. Hence, in order to move toward a critical practice of bicultural education, it is most important to examine the fundamental theoretical dimensions behind critical education and their merit in respect to the education of bicultural students.

In the spirit of a critical theory, it is important to begin by stating that there does not exist a recipe for the universal implementation and application of any form of critical pedagogy. In fact, it is precisely this distinguishing characteristic that constitutes its genuinely critical nature, and therefore its emancipatory and democratic function. This quality is consistent with the philosophical principles espoused by major critical theorists over the years. Those theorists who have most influenced the critical theory movement include members of the Frankfurt School, Italian Marxist Antonio Gramsci, and more recently

Jurgen Habermas (1970). Two of the most significant educational theorists who have built on the work of Adorno, Marcuse, Horkheimer, and others include Paulo Freire and Henry Giroux. Hence, much of current critical education theory has been profoundly influenced by these two educational philosophers—a fact that will be quite evident in the following discussion of critical pedagogy.

Cultural Politics

Above all things, a critical pedagogy must encompass an unwavering commitment to empower the powerless and transform existing social inequities and injustices (McLaren, 1988). This commitment is clearly linked to a basic principle that we as men and women are called to struggle for: what Freire (1970) defines as our "vocation"—to be truly humanized social agents in the world. This spirit of social justice moves the critical educator to an irrevocable commitment to the oppressed and to the liberation of all people.

Prior to continuing with this discussion on critical pedagogy, it is important to distinguish the concept of *pedagogy* from that of teaching. Roger Simon describes this distinction:

Pedagogy is a more complex and extensive term than teaching, referring to the integration in practice of particular curriculum content and design, classroom strategies and techniques, a time and place for the practice of these . . . and evaluation purpose and methods. All of these aspects of educational practice come together in the realities of what happens in classrooms. Together they organize a view of how teachers' work within an institutional context specifies a particular version of what knowledge is of most worth, what it means to know something, and how we might construct representations of ourselves, others, and our physical and social environment. In other words, talk about pedagogy is simultaneously talk about details of what students and others might do together and the cultural politics such practices support. To propose a pedagogy is to propose a political vision. In this perspective, we cannot talk about teaching practices without talking about politics. (Simon, 1987, p. 371)

In light of the above definition, a major task of critical educational theory is to expose and challenge the roles that schools play

in the political and cultural life of students. Of particular importance is a critical analysis and investigation into the manner that
traditional theories and practices of American schools have
thwarted or supported the participation of bicultural students.
Hence, schools must be seen critically as both sorting mechanisms
in which select groups of students are entitled in respect to race,
class, and gender, and as agencies for social and self-empowerment (McLaren, 1988).

Fundamental to critical pedagogy is the assumption that
teachers must understand the role schooling plays in uniting
knowledge and power, and how this dynamic relates to the
development of critically thinking and socially active individuals.
Unlike the traditional educational perspective that views schools
as neutral and apolitical in nature, a critical theoretical perspective views power, politics, history, and culture as intimately and
ideologically linked with any theory of education. McLaren (1988)
writes in *Life in Schools: An Introduction to Critical Pedagogy
in the Foundation of Education:* "[S]chools have always functioned
in ways that rationalize the knowledge industry into class-divided
tiers; that reproduce inequality, racism, and sexism; and that fragment democratic social relations through an emphasis on competitiveness and ethnocentrism" (pp. 160–161).

Critical pedagogy incorporates Freire's (1970) notion that the
form and content of knowledge, as well as the social practices
through which it is appropriated, have to be seen as an ongoing
struggle over what counts as legitimate culture and forms of empowerment. In accordance with this notion, a critical pedagogy
must seriously address the concept of cultural politics by both
legitimizing and challenging cultural experiences that comprise
the histories and social realities that in turn comprise the forms
and boundaries that give meaning to the lives of students.

Economics

Critical education theory also fiercely challenges the prevalent
assumption that the function of American schools is based on the
broad Western humanistic tradition for individual and social empowerment. In fact, it contends that, in truth, schools often work
against the interests of those students who are most in need of

No lo creo

these opportunities. Consequently, the issue of economics is considered vital to developing a critical understanding of how school curriculum, knowledge, and policy are organized around the inequity of competing interests within the social order and thus are dependent on the corporate marketplace and the success of the national economy.

Critical theorists maintain a view of schooling as a cultural and historical process in which select groups are positioned within asymmetrical relations of power on the basis of specific race, class, and gender groups, rather than a process that is value-free and neutral. Its political dimensions are sharply defined within the argument that schools often operate with the intent to reproduce the values and privileges of the dominant culture. McLaren (1988) speaks to this: "Critical theorists challenge the often uncontested relationship between school and society, unmasking mainstream pedagogy's claim that it purveys equal opportunity and provides access to egalitarian democracy and critical thinking. Critical scholars reject the claim that schooling constitutes an apolitical and value-neutral process" (p. 163).

As discussed earlier, nowhere is this form of inequity so clearly evident as in the current system of meritocracy utilized in most American schools—a system that, in order to succeed, requires students to be versed in the dominant cultural versions of truth and knowledge. Those who succeed are considered to possess the individual merit that consequently also makes them privilege to the economic goods that success can bring in the United States. Those who fail are considered to lack the individual intelligence, maturity, or drive to succeed. Seldom acknowledged in this traditional analysis of student success or failure are the asymmetrical power relations determined by cultural and economic forces that grant privilege to students from the dominant culture.

Historicity of Knowledge

Critical pedagogy is strongly influenced by the Frankfurt School's notion of the *historicity of knowledge*. True to this underlying principle, the theory calls for the examination of schools within not only their social practices but also their historical realities. Herein lies a counterlogic to the positivist, ahistorical, and depoliticizing analysis of schooling that searches for *inner histories* within a specific historical context. With respect to this view, Giroux argues that

[the] given social order is not simply found in modes of interpretation that view history as a natural evolving process or ideologies distributed through the culture industry. It is also found in the material reality of those needs and wants that bear the inscription of history. That is, history is to be found as "second nature" in those concepts and views of the world that make the most dominating aspect of the social order appear to be immune from historical sociopolitical development. Those aspects of reality that rest on an appeal to the universal and invariant often slip from historical consciousness and become embedded within those historically specific needs and desires that link individuals to the logic of conformity and domination. (Giroux, 1983, p. 38)

Critical educational theorists strongly support the view that the study of history, which has deteriorated at all levels of schooling, must be elevated to a position of critical influence. However, instead of orienting the curriculum to a patriotic purpose that stresses the role of great men in shaping our contemporary world, or featuring events whose meaning is usually lost to students, educators should assist students in understanding history as a social process—a process that incorporates both the participation of social movements and the state, as well as the economic and cultural forces acting as significant determinants in the society. Further, since historical events often conceal more than they reveal, the issue of historical understanding is also closely predicated on deconstructing events, texts, and images of the past. Within this context, the meaning of history is to be found not only in what is included in mainstream explanations, but also in what is excluded (Aronowitz & Giroux, 1985).

Important to this discussion is the manner in which the dominant school culture functions not only to support the interests and values of the dominant society, but also to marginalize and invalidate knowledge forms and experiences that are significant to subordinate and oppressed groups. This function is best illustrated in the ways that curriculum often blatantly ignores the histories of women, people of color, and the working classes. Freire (1970)

Historia: de los opprimidos

speaks to the impact of this historical neglect of oppressed groups:
"There is no historical reality which is not human. There is no
history without men [sic], and no history for men; there is only
history of men, made by men and . . . in turn making them. It is
when the majorities are denied their right to participate in history
as subjects that they become dominated and alienated" (p. 125).

With this in mind, a critical pedagogical approach must appropriate students' own histories by delving into their own
biographies and systems of meaning. But this can only take place
if the conditions are created in the classroom for students to speak
their own voices and to name and authenticate their own experiences. This is vital to the learning process, for not until
students can "become aware of the dignity of their own perceptions and histories [can they] make a leap to the theoretical and
begin to examine the truth value of their meanings and perceptions, particularly as they relate to the dominant rationality"
(Giroux, 1983, p. 203).

Hence, unlike traditional discourses on education, a critical
perspective opposes the positivist emphasis on historical con-
tinuities and historical development. In its place is found a mode
of analysis that stresses the breaks, discontinuities, and tensions
in history, all of which become valuable in that they highlight the
centrality of human agency and struggle while simultaneously
revealing the gap between society as it presently exists and society
as it might be (Giroux, 1983).

Dialectical Theory

Unlike traditional theories of education that seek certainty and
the technical control of knowledge and power, critical education
theory posits a dialectical notion of knowledge that seeks to un-
cover the connections between objective knowledge and the
norms, values, and structural relationships of the wider society.
As such, it provides students with a mode of engagement that
permits them to examine the underlying political, social, and
economic contexts in which they live.

A dialectical view[1] begins with the fact of human existence and
the contradictions and disjunctions that, in part, shape it and make
problematic its meaning in the world. It functions to assist

students to analyze their world, to become aware of the limitations that prevent them from changing the world, and, finally, to help them collectively struggle to transform that world. McLaren describes this process:

Critical [pedagogy] begin[s] with the premise that men and women are essentially unfree and inhabit a world rife with contradictions and asymmetries of power and privilege. The critical educator endorses theories that are, first and foremost, dialectical: that is, theories which recognize the problems of society as more than simply isolated events of individuals or deficiencies in the social structure. Rather, these problems are part of the interactive context between the individual and society. (McLaren, 1988, p. 166)

Dialectical thought seeks out these social contradictions and sets up a process of open and thoughtful questioning that requires reflection to ensue back and forth between the parts and the whole, the object and the subject, knowledge and human action, process and product, so that further contradictions may be discovered. As these are revealed, new constructive forms of thinking and action are necessary to transcend the original state. The complement of elements is dynamic rather than fixed or static and results in a form of tension rather than a state of polarization. Thus, within a dialectic, the elements are regarded as mutually constitutive rather than separate and distinct (McLaren, 1988).

Significant to a dialectical understanding of education is a view of schools as sites of both oppression and empowerment. Here, the traditional view of schools as neutral, value-free sites that provide students with the necessary skills and attitudes for becoming good and responsible citizens in society is clearly rejected. Instead, this view argues for a partisan perspective that is fundamentally committed to a struggle for the transformation of society based on the principles of emancipatory education, which are realized only through nonexploitative relations and social justice. Within this context, the contradictions that result within undemocratic forms of relationships are perceived as a multitude of questions that must be explored with students to reveal how they are linked to class, gender, and race interests (McLaren, 1988).

Dialectical thought reveals the power of human activity and human knowledge as both a product of and force in the shaping of social reality. Further, it argues that there is a link between knowledge, power, and domination. Therefore, it recognizes that some knowledge is false, and that the ultimate purpose of a dialectical critique is critical thinking in the interest of social change. It is important to note that, consequently, critical thought can be exercised without falling into the ideological trap of relativism, in which the notion of critique is negated by the assumption that all ideas should be considered equally.

Giroux (1981) elaborates further on this notion of dialectics in *Ideology, Culture, and the Process of Schooling:* "The dialectic incorporates an historical sensibility in the interest of liberating human beings not only from those traditions that legitimate oppressive institutional arrangements, but also from their own history, i.e., that which society has made of them. This is the critical point that links praxis and historical consciousness" (p. 118).

Critical theorists argue that what is needed to unravel the source, mechanisms, and elements that constitute the fabric of school culture is a theory of *dialectical critique*. Based on Adorno's (1973) notion of *negative dialectics*, it begins with a rejection of traditional representations of reality. The underlying assumption is that critical reflection is formed out of the principles of negativity, contradiction, and mediation. This calls for a thorough interrogation of all universal "truths" and social practices that go unquestioned in schools because they are concealed in the guise of objectivity and neutrality (Giroux, 1983).

Hence, the primary purpose of a dialectical critique within the context of a critical pedagogy is to address two concerns: (1) the linking of social experiences with the development of modes of criticism that can interrogate such experiences and reveal both their strengths and weaknesses; and (2) the presentation of a mode of praxis fashioned in new critical thought aimed at reclaiming the conditions of self-determined existence.

Praxis: The Union of Theory and Practice

Critical educational theory, in all respects, encompasses a practical intent that is fundamentally centered around the practical transformation of the world. It is this basic interest in the human condition—never seen as separate from the development and liberation of self-consciousness of individuals actively involved with determining their own destiny—that is at the heart of a critical pedagogy. Unlike the external determinism, pragmatism, and instrumental/technical application of theory so prevalent in traditional American educational discourses, *praxis is conceived as self-creating and self-generating free human action*. Freire (1970) makes reference to this notion of praxis: "The difference between animals–who . . . cannot create products detached from themselves—and men [and women]—who through their action upon the world create the realm of culture and history—is that only the latter are beings of praxis. . . . It is as transforming and creating beings that men, in their permanent relations with reality, produce" (pp. 90–91).

Within this view of human beings, all human activity consists of action and reflection, or praxis. And as praxis, all human activity requires theory to illuminate it. This interface between theory and practice occurs, for example, at the point where oppressed groups come together and raise fundamental questions of how they might assist each other, and how—through such an exchange of views—an action might emerge in which all groups might benefit. But it is crucial to note, once again, that this does not suggest that all views are to be given equal weight, for such a view could easily degenerate into relativistic nonsense. Instead, what it suggests is that the human subject must be integrated into the process of theorizing, and that truth claims of specific theoretical perspectives must be analyzed and mediated through dialogue and democratic social relations. Central, then, to this interface of theory and practice is the fundamental notion of *critique* (Giroux, 1983).

From the standpoint of a critical pedagogical perspective, we can further examine the dialectical relationship between theory and practice in respect to the concrete and theoretical contexts. In the *concrete* context, students can be perceived as subjects and objects in a dialectical relationship with reality. In the *theoretical* context, they play the role of cognitive subjects of the subject-object relationship that occurs in the concrete context. In this way, they are able to return to a place where they can better react as subjects against reality. This represents a vital point in the unity between theory and practice (Freire, 1985).

Further, it is only as *beings of praxis*—as students accept their concrete situations as a challenging condition—that they are able to change its meaning by their action. This is why Freire (1985) argues that a true praxis is impossible in the undialectical vacuum where we are driven by a subject/object dichotomy. For within the context of such a dichotomy, both theory and practice lose their power to transform reality. Cut off from practice, theory becomes simple verbalism. Separated from theory, practice is nothing but blind activism. Thus, authentic praxis can only occur where there exists a dialectical union between theory and practice.

However, it is important to note that, although critical pedagogy incorporates the union of theory and practice in education, this does not mean theory and practice—while interconnected at the point of experience—are considered identical in character. Rather, to the contrary, they represent distinct analytical moments and should not collapse into each other (Horkheimer, 1972). Giroux also addresses this notion:

Theory must be celebrated for its truth content, not for the methodological refinements it employs. . . . [T]heory is informed by practice; but its real value lies in its ability to provide the reflexivity needed to interpret the concrete experience. . . . Theory can never be reduced to practice, because the specificity of practice has its own center of theoretical gravity, and cannot be reduced to a predefined formula. That is, the specificity of practice cannot be abstracted from the complex forces, struggles, and mediations that give each situation a unique defining quality. Theory can help us understand this quality, but cannot reduce it to the logic of a mathematical formula. . . . Experience and concrete studies do not speak for themselves, and . . . will tell us very little if the theoretical framework we use to interpret them lacks depth and critical rigor. (Giroux, 1983, pp. 99–100)

Ideology

Critical educational theorists conceive of ideology as the framework of thought which is used in society to give order and meaning to the social and political world (Hall, 1981). The notion of ideology cannot be ignored within the context of a critical pedagogy, for it defines for students the perceptual field from which to make sense of the world. As described earlier, ideology not only structures our perceptions, but also gives meaning and direction to all we experience. McLaren (1988) defines ideology as

the production and representation of ideas, values, and beliefs and the manner in which they are expressed and lived out by both individuals and groups. . . . [I]deology refers to the production of sense and meaning. It can be described as a way of viewing the world, a complex of ideas, various types of social practices, rituals, and representations that are accepted as natural and as common sense. It is the result of the intersection of meaning and power in the social world. (p. 176)

Utilizing the Frankfurt School's notion of depth psychology, critical educational theorists see ideology as existing in the depth of the individual's psychological structure of needs. This supports the view that critical educators must take into account students' inner histories and experiences, they being central to questions of subjectivity as they are constructed by individual needs, drives, passions, and intelligence, as well as changing political, economic, and social foundations of the wider society. But further, ideology is also seen as existing in the realm of common sense. Here, *common sense* refers to the level of everyday consciousness with its many forms of unexamined assumptions, moral codes, contradictions, and partial truths (Giroux, 1981).

Also essential to a critical theory of education is the notion that ideology provides individuals with the means for critique. This occurs through its own structure of thought processes and practical activities. Hence, ideology becomes a critical pedagogical tool when it is used to interrogate the relationship between the dominant school culture and the contradictory lived experiences that mediate the reality of school life. Within this context, Giroux argues that three important distinctions provide the foundation for a theory of ideology and classroom practice:

First, a distinction must be made between theoretical and practical ideologies. . . . [T]heoretical ideologies refer to the beliefs and values embedded in the categories that teachers and students use to shape and interpret the pedagogical process, while practical ideologies refer to the

messages and norms embedded in classroom social relations and practices. Second, a distinction must be made between discourse and lived
experience as instances of ideology and as the material grounding of
ideology as they are embedded in school texts, films, and other cultural
artifacts that make up visual and aural media. Third, these ideological
elements gain part of their significance only as they are viewed in their
articulation with the broader relations of society. (Giroux, 1983, p. 67)

One implication for classroom practice to be drawn from a
theory of ideology is that it provides teachers with a context to
examine how their own views about knowledge, human nature,
values, and society are mediated through the commonsense
assumptions they use to structure classroom experiences. Here,
the concept of ideology provides a starting point for asking questions about the social and political interests and values that inform many of the pedagogical assumptions teachers take for
granted in their work. Educators must evaluate critically their
assumptions about learning, achievement, teacher–student relations, objectivity, and school authority.

Further, critical educational theorists support the notion that
ideology as critique must also be used to investigate classroom
relations that freeze the spirit of critical inquiry among students.
These pedagogical practices must be measured against the potential to foster rather than hamper intellectual growth and social
inquiry. This becomes particularly important for those students
who experience daily humiliation and a sense of powerlessness
due to the fact that their own lived experiences and cultural
histories are in conflict with the dominant school culture (Giroux,
1983).

Ideology as critique is also an essential tool that can be used
by teachers to understand how the dominant culture becomes
embedded in the hidden curriculum. Understanding how curriculum materials and other artifacts produce meaning assists
teachers in decoding the messages inscribed in both form and content. This is particularly significant in light of the results gathered
by content analysis studies (e.g., Pokewitz, 1978; Anyon, 1979,
1980) that consistently reveal the prominence of dominant cultural
values reflected in the majority of textbooks and curricula utilized in American schools.

Another significant factor in the production of self-awareness in teachers is the ability to decode and critique the ideologies inscribed in the form of structuring principles behind the presentation of images in curriculum materials. The significant silences of a text must be uncovered. Teachers must learn to identify the ideological messages in texts that focus on individuals to the exclusion of collective action, that juxtapose high culture and structures that reproduce poverty and exploitation, or that use forms of discourse that do not promote critical engagement by students (Giroux, 1983).

Critical educational theorists argue for a view of the hidden curriculum that encompasses all the ideological instances of the schooling process that silence students and structurally reproduce the dominant society's assumptions and practices. Such a focus is important because it shifts the emphasis away from a preoccupation with reproducing the status quo to a primary concern for cultural intervention and social action.

Hegemony

Critical pedagogy incorporates Gramsci's (1971) view that educators need to understand how the dominant worldview and its social practices are produced throughout society in order to shatter the mystification of the existing power relationships and social arrangements that sustain them. Through his theory of hegemony, Gramsci argues that there exists a powerful interconnection between politics, cultural ideology, and pedagogy.

Hegemony, as previously discussed, is systematically carried out through the moral and intellectual leadership of a dominant society over subordinate groups. This form of societal control is achieved not through physically coercive means nor arbitrary rules or regulations, but rather through winning the consent of the subordinated to the authority of the dominant class. The dominant society does not need to impose hegemony by force, since the oppressed actively subscribe to many of the values and objectives of the dominant class without being aware of the source of those values or the interests that inform them. Through hegemonic control, the dominant culture is able to exert domination over women, people of color, and members of the working class. This process occurs whenever relations of power established at the institutional level are systematically asymmetrical—that is, when they are unequal and therefore grant privilege to some groups over others.

Given this view, teachers practice hegemony when they fail to teach their students how to question the prevailing social attitudes, values, and social practices of the dominant society in a sustained, critical manner. Thus, the challenge for teachers is to recognize, critique, and attempt to transform those undemocratic and oppressive features of hegemonic control that structure classroom experiences in ways that are not readily apparent (McLaren, 1985).

Critical educators recognize that hegemony, in whatever form that it manifests in society, must be fought for constantly in order to maintain the status quo. This, however difficult, is most successfully accomplished through various forms of co-optational forces that are constantly at work in the classroom and the society at large. But despite this oppressive quality, Giroux (1981) points to another significant aspect for critical educators. He argues that a theory of hegemony can also serve as an important pedagogical tool for understanding both the prevailing modes of domination and the ensuing contradictions and tensions existing within such modes of control. In this way, hegemony can function as a theoretical basis for helping teachers to understand not only how the seeds of domination are produced, but also how they may be overcome through various forms of resistance, critique, and social action.

Resistance and Counter-hegemony

Critical pedagogy incorporates a theory of resistance in order to understand better the complex reasons why many students from subordinate groups consistently fail in the educational system, and how this understanding may be used to restructure classroom practices and relationships as a form of *counter-hegemony*: "an alternative public sphere that is clearly guided by emancipatory interests" (Giroux & McLaren, 1987, p. 64)

Critical educators adhere to the philosophical principle that all people have the capacity to make meaning of their lives and to resist oppression. But they also recognize the fact that the capacity to resist and understand is limited and influenced by issues of class, race, and gender. People will use whatever means at hand or whatever power they can employ to meet their needs and assert their humanity. But, unfortunately, since the solutions they often select arise from the ascribed beliefs and values of the dominant society, they may in fact lead themselves and others deeper into forms of domination and oppression (Weiler, 1985).

Giroux (1983) has addressed extensively this notion of resistance by suggesting that a construct of resistance points to a number of assumptions and concerns generally unexamined by traditional views of schooling:

First, it celebrates a dialectical notion of human agency that rightly portrays domination as neither a static process nor one that is ever complete[; similarly,] the oppressed are not viewed as being simply passive. [It] points to the need to understand more thoroughly [how] people mediate and respond to the interface between their own lived experiences and the structures of domination. . . . Secondly, resistance adds . . . depth to Foucault's (1977) notion that power works so as to be exercised on and by people within different contexts that structure interacting relations of dominance and autonomy. . . . [P]ower is never unidimensional. . . . Finally, inherent in the notion of resistance is an expressed hope, an element of transcendence, for radical transformation. (Giroux, 1983, p. 108)

Central to a critical theory of resistance is the concern with uncovering the degree to which a student's oppositional act speaks to a form of refusal that expresses the need to struggle against elements of dehumanization. From this context, an understanding of resistance serves a critical function in analyzing behavior based on the specific historical and relational conditions from which it develops. This is vital to the process of critical pedagogy, for—without this process of critical inquiry—resistance could easily be allowed to become a category indiscriminately assigned to all forms of student oppositional behavior. It is the notion of emancipatory interests that must be central to determining when oppositional behavior constitutes a moment of resistance.

The pedagogical value of resistance is clearly linked to notions of structure and human agency and the concept of culture and self-formation, and situating these in a new problematic for understanding the process of schooling. Giroux speaks to this concept of resistance:

> It rejects a notion that schools are simply instructional sites, and in so doing, it not only politicizes the notion of culture [and ideology], but also points to the need to analyze school culture within the shifting terrain of struggle and contestation. Educational knowledge, values, and social relations are now placed within the context of lived antagonistic relations, and the need to be examined as they are played out within the dominant and subordinate cultures that characterize school life. (Giroux, 1983, p. 111)

Hence, elements of resistance are emphasized within a critical educational perspective in an effort to construct different sets of lived experiences—experiences in which students can find a voice and maintain and extend the positive aspects of their own social and historical realities. Freire and Macedo comment on the importance of this function of resistance for the critical educator:

> Understanding the oppressed's reality, as reflected in the various forms of cultural production—language, music, art—leads to a better comprehension of the cultural expression through which people articulate their rebelliousness against the dominant. These cultural expressions [of resistance] also represent the level of possible struggle against oppression. . . . [A]ny radical educator must first understand fully the dynamics of resistance on the part of learners . . . to better understand the discourse of resistance, to provide pedagogical structures that will enable students to emancipate themselves. (Freire and Macedo, 1987, pp. 137–38)

At this point, it is necessary to recall that, at times, despite the well-intentioned interventions of critical educators, there are students whose oppositional behavior is directed toward holding firm to their hegemonic views of the world. Brian Fay (1987) explains that, having internalized the values, beliefs, and even worldview of the dominant class, these students resist seeing themselves as oppressed, and so they willingly cooperate with those who oppress them by maintaining social practices that perpetuate their subordinate position. Freire identifies this phenomenon as the initial stage of emancipation, where the oppressed, instead of striving for liberation, tend themselves to become oppressors. . . . [T]he very structure of their thought has been conditioned by the contradictions of the concrete, existential situation by which they were shaped. . . . This phenomenon derives from the fact that the oppressed, at a certain moment of their experience, adopt an attitude of adhesion to the oppressor. . . . [T]heir perception of themselves as oppressed is impaired by their submersion in the reality of oppression. . . . [T]he oppressed find in the oppressor their model. (Freire, 1970, pp. 29–30)

Thus, in light of the forms that resistance takes in the lives of oppressed students, the starting point of any counter-hegemonic pedagogy must be the world of these students, from the standpoint both of their oppression and their opposition. Essential to this process is the struggle for counter-hegemony and a movement toward more democratic institutional relationships and alternative value systems that are based on a critical understanding of the world and an overriding commitment to the inherent emancipatory nature of human beings.

Critical Discourse

An understanding of the power dynamics that embody the notion of discourse is essential to an understanding of the purpose that underlies critical pedagogy. For what critical pedagogy represents, in actuality, is an effort to develop a critical discourse in the face of a dominant discourse that has worked systematically to silence the voices of women, people of color, and other oppressed groups in the United States.

Discourse is derived as a system of discursive practices that reflect the values, beliefs, ideology, language, and economic constraints found within a particular set of inscribed power relations. As such, discursive practices refer to the rules by which discourses are formed, and thus determine what can be said and what must remain unsaid, who can speak with authority and who must listen. Hence, discourses and discursive practices influence how we live out our lives. They shape our subjective experiences, because it is primarily through language and discourse that social reality is given meaning (McLaren, 1988).

Critical educational theorists argue that, since knowledge is socially constructed, culturally mediated, and historically situated, dominant discourses function to determine what is relegated to the arenas of truth and relevancy at any given moment in time. Thus, they hold a view of truth as relational, in that statements considered true are seen as arising within a particular context, based on the relations of power operative in a society, discipline, or institution. This helps to explain why only those discourses that accommodate to the power relations prescribed by the dominant discourse are generally acknowledged, and how these are clearly linked to the question of what they produce and in whose interest they function (Freire, 1985).

Consequently, critical discourse must focus on those interests and assumptions that inform the generation of knowledge itself. But true to its emancipatory principles, it must also be self-critical and deconstructive of dominant discourses the moment they are ready to solidify into hegemonic knowledge. In this way, critical pedagogy can work to replace the "authoritarian discourse of imposition and recitation with a voice capable of speaking one's own terms, a voice capable of listening, retelling, and challenging the very grounds of knowledge and power" (Freire & Macedo, 1987, p. 20).

Critical pedagogy relegates to critical reason the possibility of establishing the conditions of discourse for the raising and reconciling of controversial claims related to knowledge and power. Here, *critical reason* stands for liberation from all regulations of social intercourse and interactions that suppress the debatability of truth (Forester, 1987).

Many critical theorists turn to Habermas's (1970) theory of *practical discourse* and the *ideal speech situation* for a rational standard by which to judge existing discourses. Such a standard suggests that a system of communication can only be free from both internal and external constraints when all participants to a discourse possess equal opportunity to select and use speech acts. John Forester describes the process as having the following four requirements for all potential participants:

1. the same chance to employ communication speech acts, that is, to initiate and perpetuate the discourse. . . .

2. the same chance to employ representative speech acts to express attitudes, feelings, and intentions. . . .

3. equal chance to use regulative speech acts; they must be equally able to command and oppose, permit, and forbid arguments. They must also have equal opportunity to both make and accept promises and provide and call for justifications. . . .

4. equal opportunity to provide interpretations and explanations and also to problematize any validity claims so that in the long run no one view is exempt from consideration and criticism. (Forester, 1987, pp. 186–88)

What this concept clearly suggests to critical educational theorists is that respecting different discourses and putting into practice a theory committed to the plurality of voices will require nothing short of political and social transformation. Given this reality, *critical discourse as a transformative act* must assume an active and decisive participation relative to what is produced and for whom. Freire and Macedo address this notion in relation to the *reinvention of power*:

The reinvention of power that passes through the reinvention of production would entail the reinvention of culture within which environments would be created to incorporate, in a participatory way, all of those discourses that are presently suffocated by the dominant discourse. [This] legitimation of these different discourses would authenticate the plurality of voices in the reconstruction of a truly democratic society. (Freire and Macedo, 1987, p. 55)

Critical pedagogy addresses this transformative requirement through a discourse that rigorously unites the language of critique with the language of possibility. Here, Giroux (1985) calls for a process of schooling in which educators as *transformative intellectuals* recognize their ability to transform critically the world. In so doing, educators can carry out a counter-hegemonic project as they work to challenge economic, political, and social injustices, both within and outside schools. At the same time, teachers can work to create the conditions that give students an active voice in their learning, and support their development as social agents who have the knowledge and courage to struggle for a discourse of hope, as they also struggle to overcome the discourse of despair that is so often found in the lives of both teachers and students of subordinate cultural communities.

Dialogue and Conscientization

Critical theorists unwaveringly support the Freirian notion of dialogue as an emancipatory educational process—a process that, above all, is dedicated to the empowerment of students through disconfirming the dominant ideology of the traditional educational discourse and illuminating the freedom of students to act on their world.

For critical educators, dialogue is never perceived as a mere technique to be utilized for appropriating students' affections or obedience. Instead, it is perceived as an educational strategy committed to the development of their critical consciousness; it is a process of *conscientization*. Freire defines his notion of dialogue in *A Pedagogy for Liberation* (Shor & Freire, 1987) using the following terms:

Dialogue must be understood as something taking part in the historical nature of human beings. It is part of our historical process in becoming human beings. . . . [D]ialogue is a moment where human beings meet to reflect on their reality as they make and remake it. . . . [T]hrough dialogue, reflecting together on what we know and don't know, we can act critically to transform reality. (pp. 98–99)

This dialogical method represents the basis for a critical pedagogical structure in which dialogue and analysis serve as the foundation for reflection and action. It is an educational strategy that clearly supports the principles of what Freire (1970) calls a *problem-posing educational approach*: an approach in which the relationship of students and teachers is, without question, dialogical—students learn from teachers; teachers must also learn from students. The content of this form of education takes into account the concrete lived experiences of the students themselves as the historical character of their experiences are explored through questions that often begin, "How did we come to be what we are?" And, "How could we change?" In this way, critical educators encourage the free and uncoerced exchange of ideas and experiences. They demonstrate a caring for their students and provide them with emotional support to help them overcome their feelings of inadequacy and guilt as they become critics of the social world they inhabit (Fay, 1987).

What dialogue, then, represents is a human phenomenon in which students, with the guidance of the teacher, move into a discovery of themselves as social agents. It is through their encounter with reality that they are supported and yet challenged to assess their world critically and to unmask the central contradictions of their existence. And, in so doing, by way of praxis—the authentic union of their action and reflection—they enter into a process of conscientization.

For Freire (Shor & Freire, 1987), conscientization refers to the process by which students—not as recipients of knowledge, but as knowing subjects—achieve a deepening awareness of the sociopolitical and economic realities that shape their lives and their capacity to recreate them. This implies the critical insertion of a conscientized individual into a demythologized reality. It is this state of conscientization that assists students to transform their apathy—formerly nourished by their disempowerment—into the *denunciation* of the previous reality and their *annunciation* into a viable, transformed existence. Further, conscientization is conceived as a recurrent, regenerating process that is utilized for constant clarification of what remains hidden within, while students continue to move into the world and enter into dialogue anew.

A CRITICAL BICULTURAL PEDAGOGY

From the above discussion of critical pedagogy, it is clearly evident that the theoretical constructs that constitute a critical perspective of education are also highly conducive to the educational needs of bicultural students. Coupled with a political construct of cultural democracy, this critical dimension can effectively provide a foundation for a liberatory practice of bicultural education that can genuinely prepare Black, Latino, Asian, Native American, and other bicultural students to become transformative agents in their world.

A critical bicultural pedagogy holds the possibility for a discourse of hope in light of the tensions, conflicts, and contradictions that students must face in the process of their bicultural development. A practice that is based on this framework of critical bicultural education will provide for students the opportunity to explore their own world as they seek also to understand how the dominant culture affects their lives and how they view themselves as human beings.

Through an understanding of hegemony and cultural invasion, critical bicultural educators can create culturally democratic environments where they can assist students to identify the different ways that domination and oppression have an impact on their lives. Through a process of dialogue, all students can examine and compare together the content of historical texts with their own personal and cultural histories and come to understand their role as social agents in society. In this way, bicultural students can also begin to experience democratic participation as part of their lived histories as they develop together a spirit of solidarity and an understanding of the common good.

A critical bicultural pedagogy can also create the conditions for bicultural students to develop the courage to question the structures of domination that control their lives. In this way, they can awaken their bicultural voice as they participate in opportunities to reflect, critique, and act together with other bicultural students who are also experiencing the same process of discovery. Hence, these students are not just provided with curricular content that is considered culturally appropriate and language instruction in their native tongues. Rather, they are actively involved in considering critically all curriculum content, texts, classroom experiences, and their own lives for the emancipatory as well as oppressive and contradictory values that inform their thoughts, attitudes, and behaviors. Through this process, bicultural students develop their abilities to understand critically their lives and how to engage actively in the world.

If bicultural students are to succeed in American schools, critical bicultural educators must accept a commitment to work in transforming the traditionally oppressive structures of educational institutions and to struggle with bicultural students so they may truly become beings for themselves. In summary, this can be best accomplished through a critical bicultural pedagogy that

1. is built on a theory of cultural democracy;
2. supports a dialectical view of the world, particularly as it relates to the notion of culture and the bicultural experience;
3. recognizes those forms of cultural invasion that negatively influence the lives of bicultural students and their families;
4. utilizes a dialogical model of communication that can create the conditions for students of color to find their voice through opportunities to reflect, critique, and act on their world to transform it;
5. acknowledges the issue of power in society and the political nature of schooling; and
6. above all, is committed to the empowerment and liberation of all people.

NOTE

1. For an excellent introduction to the historical and philosophical roots of dialectical theory, see *The Emergence of Dialectical Theory* (Warren, 1984).

CHAPTER 5

CREATING THE CONDITIONS
FOR CULTURAL DEMOCRACY
IN THE CLASSROOM

But democracy, by definition, cannot mean merely that an unskilled worker can become skilled. It must mean that every "citizen" can "govern" and that society places him [or her] in a general condition to achieve this.

Antonio Gramsci
Selections from Prison Notebooks

Cultural democracy in the classroom cannot be discussed, within the context of a critical bicultural pedagogy, outside of the theoretical dimensions that function to position teachers with respect to their educational practice. Gramsci's words support a theory of cultural democracy that not only locates bicultural students within a historical and cultural context, but also addresses questions related to moral and political agency within the process of their schooling and the course of their everyday lives. In short, this critical view suggests that, prior to any engagement with instrumental questions of practice, educators must delve rigorously into those specific theoretical issues that are fundamental to the establishment of a culturally democratic foundation for a critical bicultural pedagogy in the classroom.

This view is also consistent with that of Freire (1970) and other critical educational theorists who emphatically express that any liberatory pedagogy cannot represent a recipe for classroom practice. Rather, it is meant to provide a set of critical educational principles that can guide and support teachers' critical engagement with the forces determining the reality of classroom life. Informed by this tradition, a critical foundation for bicultural education must not be presented in the form of models for duplication or how-to instruction manuals. One of the most important reasons for this thinking is expressed by Simon (1988), who speaks eloquently to the notion that all educational practice must emerge from the contextual relationships defined by the very conditions existing at any given moment within the classroom. Such a practice "is at root contextual and conditional. A critical pedagogy can only be concretely discussed from within a particular 'point of practice,' from within a specific time and place, and within a particular theme" (p. 1).

Hence, efforts to instrumentalize or operationalize a critical perspective outside the context in which it is to function fails to engage with the historical, cultural, and dialogical principles that are essential to a critical learning environment. In addition, this approach also ignores that, prior to the development of practice, there are cultural and ideological assumptions at work determining how educators define the purpose of education, their role, and the role of their students in the process of schooling. The belief that teachers must be provided with "canned" curriculum to ensure their success fails to acknowledge the creative potential of educators to grapple effectively with the multiplicity of contexts that they find in their classrooms and to shape environments according to the lived experiences and actual educational needs of their students.

Teacher education programs are notorious for reducing the role of teachers to that of technicians. Instead of empowering teachers by assisting them to develop a critical understanding of their purpose as educators, most programs foster a dependency on predefined curriculum, outdated classroom strategies and techniques, and traditionally rigid classroom environments that position not only students but teachers as well into physically and intellectually oppressive situations. This occurs to such a degree that few public school teachers are able to envision their practice outside the scope of barren classroom settings, lifeless instructional packages, bland textbooks, standardized tests, and the use of meritocratic systems for student performance evaluation.

Educators of bicultural students must recognize the manner in which these conditions work to disempower both teachers and students in American public schools. Teachers can then begin to refuse the role of technicians in their practice as educators as they struggle together to abandon their dependency on traditional classroom artifacts. This represents an essential step if teachers are to educate students of color to discover themselves and their potential within an environment that permits them to interact with what they know to be their world. This is particularly important, given the fact that values supporting cultural diversity, social struggle, and human rights are so often absent from the curricular materials teachers are forced to use in most public schools.

A critical bicultural pedagogy that is built on a foundation of cultural democracy represents a missing educational discourse in the preparation and practice of most public school teachers. As discussed in Chapter 3, the many different forms in which the bicultural experience manifests itself in American life seldom find their way into traditional classroom settings. Instead, bicultural experiences remain, for the most part, hidden within the re-inforced silence of students of color. If the voices of difference are to find a place in the everyday interactions of public schools, educators of bicultural students must create the conditions for all students to experience an ongoing process of culturally democratic life. With this in mind, this chapter will address the major questions and issues that educators face in their efforts to pave the way for a critical bicultural pedagogy.

THE QUESTION OF LANGUAGE

It is impossible to consider any form of education—or even human existence—without first considering the impact of language on our lives. Language must be recognized as one of the most significant human resources; it functions in a multitude of ways to affirm, contradict, negotiate, challenge, transform, and empower particular cultural and ideological beliefs and practices. Language constitutes one of the most powerful media for transmitting our personal histories and social realities, as well as for thinking and shaping the world (Cole & Scribner, 1974). Language is essential to the process of dialogue, to the development of meaning, and to the production of knowledge. From the context of its emancipatory potential, language must be understood as a dialectical phenomenon that links its very existence and meaning to the lived experiences of the language community and constitutes a major cornerstone for the development of voice.

The question of language must also be addressed within the context of a terrain of struggle that is central to our efforts to transform traditional educational structures that historically have failed bicultural students. In doing so, it is essential that we do not fall into totalizing theoretical traps—ignoring that human beings are in fact able to appropriate a multitude of linguistic forms and utilize them in critical and emancipatory ways. It is simplistic and to our detriment as educators of bicultural students to accept the notion that any one particular form of language (i.e., "standard" English), in and of itself, constitutes a totalizing dominant or subordinate force, as it is unrealistic to believe that simply utilizing a student's primary language (e.g., Spanish, Ebonics, etc.) guarantees that a student's emancipatory interests are being addressed. Consequently, the question of language in the classroom constitutes one of the most complex and multifaceted issues that educators of bicultural students must be prepared to address in the course of their practice.

The complexity of language and its relationship not only to how students produce knowledge but also to how language shapes their world represent a major pedagogical concern for all educational settings. In public schools, teachers can begin to address this complexity by incorporating activities based on the languages their students bring into the classroom. In this way, the familiar language can function as a significant starting point from which bicultural students can engage with the foreign and unknown elements that comprise significant portions of the required curriculum. An example of how teachers might do this with younger students is to develop language instruction and activities with their student that give them the opportunity to bring the home language into the context of the classroom. This can be done by having students and parents introduce their languages through songs, stories, games, and other such activities. Giving attention to the home language raises it to a place of dignity and respect, rather than permitting it to become a source of humiliation and shame for bicultural students. It should be noted that the introduction of different languages must also be accompanied by critical dialogues that help students examine prevailing social attitudes and biases about language differences. These discussions can assist students to consider typical discriminatory responses to such situations as when people speak with foreign accents, or when people do not understand the language being spoken. In addition, students from similar cultural and language communities can be encouraged and made to feel comfortable when they converse together in their primary language as part of the classroom experience. Such opportunities support the development of voice, as well as affirm the bicultural experience of students of color. Bell Hooks addresses this point:

Learning to listen to different voices, hearing different speech challenges the notion that we must all assimilate—share a single similar talk—in educational institutions. Language reflects the culture from which we emerge. To deny ourselves daily use of speech patterns that are common and familiar, that embody the unique and distinctive aspect of our self is one of the ways we become estranged and alienated from our past. It is important for us to have as many languages on hand as we can know or learn. It is important for those of us who are Black, who speak in particular patois as well as standard English, to express ourselves in both ways. (Hook, 1989, pp. 79-80)

With older students, the issue of language can be addressed in more complex terms. As mentioned previously, bicultural students must find opportunities to engage in classroom dialogues and activities that permit them to explore the meaning of their lived experiences through the familiarity of their own language. But also important to their development of social consciousness and their process of conscientization is the awareness of how language and power intersect in ways that include or exclude students of color from particular social relationships. Although it is paramount that bicultural students fully develop and strengthen their bicultural voices (as Puerto Ricans, Chicanos, African-Americans, etc.) through their interactions with others in their own communities, it is also imperative that, in order to understand more fully the impact of language on social structures and practices, students of color enter into critical dialogues with those outside their cultural communities. Through the process of these cross-cultural dialogues, students come to better recognize for themselves the manner in which language works to define who they are, and how language as a tool can assist them to explore critically those possibilities that have remained hidden and out of their reach.

It is significant for teachers to recognize that it is more common for bicultural students to reflect on these issues and to express themselves predominantly through a *language of practice*—a highly pragmatic language that is primarily rooted in notions of common sense and concrete experiences. Although this process represents a necessary step in the empowerment of bicultural students, their transformative potential can only be extended when they are able to unite practice with theory, or when they are able to recognize themselves as critical beings who are constantly moving between concrete and abstract representations of experiences that influence how they make decisions about their actions in the world.

In order to create the conditions for students to determine their own lives genuinely within a multiplicity of discourses, teachers must introduce their students to the *language of theory*. The language of theory constitutes a critical language of social analysis that is produced through human efforts to understand how individuals reflect and interpret their experiences and, as a result, how they shape and are shaped by their world. Although it is a language generally connected to the realm of abstract thinking, its fundamental function of praxis cannot be fulfilled unless it is linked to the concrete experiences and practices of everyday life. Such language also encourages the use of more precise and specific linguistic representations of experience than is generally expected—or even necessary—in the course of everyday practice. Challenging bicultural students to engage openly with the language of theory and to understand better its impact on their lives can awaken them to the tremendous potential available to them as social agents.

At this point it is significant to note that what has been traditionally considered theoretical language has also been—almost exclusively—controlled and governed by those who have held power in academic circles: namely, elite, White males. As a result, the greatest number of formal theoretical texts considered as legitimate knowledge, reflect conservative, Eurocentric, patriarchal notions of the world. Generally speaking, these texts uniformly support assumptions that reinforce racism, classism and sexism, while written in such a way as to justify claims of neutrality and objectivity.

In their efforts to resist conservative forms of language domination, many educators disengage from all forms of theoretical language, thereby relegating the language of theory exclusively to a sphere of domination. Not surprisingly, this uncritical view comes dangerously close to being little more than a less recognized form of anti-intellectualism. The greatest danger is that it abandons the struggle for a liberatory language of theory by its refusal to challenge academic work that perpetuates all forms of domination and to assert the need for multiple forms of theoretical language rooted in culturally diverse perspectives and a variety of styles (Hooks, 1989).

From another standpoint, efforts to resist the inequality and alienation reinforced by traditional uses of theoretical language can result in protective mechanisms of resistance among students of color, and this too can give rise to unintentional forms of anti-intellectualism. Given the nature of such responses, it is not unusual for bicultural students, who have suffered the negative impact of domination in their lives, to reject indiscriminately those cultural forms and social institutions that they come to associate with hostility and alienation. As a consequence, it is no simple task to challenge attitudes of anti-intellectualism in the classroom. To do so requires that teachers recognize that attitudes of resistance manifested by students of color are very often rooted in legitimate fears and subsequent responses to support community survival. In addition, these fears and responses are strongly fostered by a *legacy of resistance*, which is reinforced daily through their personal and institutional relationships. These relationships include interactions with their parents, who often harbor unspoken fears that they may lose their children forever if they should become educated. Hooks describes this parental fear:

They feared what college education might do to their children's minds even as they unenthusiastically acknowledged its importance. . . . No

wonder our working class parents from poor backgrounds feared our entry into such a world, intuiting perhaps that we might learn to be ashamed
of where we had come from, that we might never return home, or come
back only to lord it over them. (Hooks, 1989, pp. 74-75)

Also included among these interactions are relationships with
many of their teachers, who themselves have never successfully
moved beyond the language of practice. Consequently, it is not
unusual for many teachers, when asked to engage with the
language of theory, to respond by feeling almost as fearful, intimidated, and disempowered as their students. Simon (forthcom-
ing) addresses this *fear of theory* among teachers who are graduate
students in his classes: "A fear of theory [is] more often expressed
by students who have had to struggle for acceptance and recognition within the dominant institutions which define the terrain of
everyday life. These are students whose lives have been lived
within the prescriptive and marginalizing effects of power
inscribed in relations of class, gender, ethnicity, race and sexual
preference" (p. 7).

These responses by teachers are often used by teacher preparation programs around the country to justify astute arguments
against the widespread use of theoretical language. More often
than not, these arguments are shaped by a lack of critical engagement with the emancipatory potential of language and by a
reproductive ideology that reduces students to simple objects who
are somehow mystically stripped of all dignity and voice by expecting them to engage in disciplined critical thought and to address abstract concepts related to practice in more precise ways.
These complaints are generally accompanied by a call for more
visual language, more anecdotal accounts, or more how-to discussions. In essence, such requests for the predominant use of a
language of practice inadvertently perpetuate a nondialectical and
dichotomized view of theory and erode the teacher's potential for
creative social action. If one listens carefully between the lines
of this pragmatic educational discourse, it echos a "false generosi-
ty of paternalism" (Freire, 1970) built on assumptions that arise
from a lack of faith in the ability of oppressed groups to appropriate, transform, and utilize the language of theory in a
liberatory fashion.

Educators in bicultural communities must grapple with their own language biases and prejudices beyond simply the issue of language differences, and work to encounter the deep frustrations and anxieties related to their fear of theory. This significant area of concern also needs to be adequately addressed by teacher preparation programs. This is particularly true for those programs that have traditionally neglected or ignored altogether this fundamental issue, as evidenced by curricula that place a greater emphasis on numerous predefined ways to teach the standard subjects rather than on exploring the complexity inherent in the human dynamics of creating meaning and producing knowledge in the classroom.

Language represents one of the most significant educational tools in our struggle for cultural democracy in the public schools. It is intimately linked to the struggle for voice, and so is essential to our struggle for liberation. Through language we not only define our position in society, but we also use that language to define ourselves as subjects in our world. Herein lies one of the most important goals for a critical bicultural pedagogy: creating the conditions for the voices of difference to find their way to the center of the dialogical process, rather than to remain forever silent or at the fringes of American classroom life.

THE QUESTION OF AUTHORITY

The question of authority represents one of the most heated areas of contention among major educational theorists in this country. This should not be surprising, for the manner in which we conceptualize authority truly represents a necessary precondition for the manner in which we define ourselves, our work, and our very lives—so much so that it is impossible to discuss cultural democracy in the classroom without addressing the issues that directly stem from this question.

In order to engage critically with the notion of authority, it is vital that teachers come to understand that authority does not automatically equal authoritarianism. Authority, within the context of a critical bicultural pedagogy, is intimately linked to the manner in which teachers exercise control, direct, influence, and make decisions about what is actually to take place in their classrooms. To engage with the question of authority in a liberatory fashion clearly requires an understanding of power and how power is used to construct relationships, define truth, and create social conditions that can potentially either subordinate or empower bicultural students. Hence, authority must be understood as a dialectical "terrain of legitimation and struggle," rather than simply as an absolute, hierarchical, and totalizing force (Giroux, 1988b).

Efforts to examine the question of authority in the classroom also require teachers to address their personal contradictions related to how they formulate ideas of control, power, and authority in their own lives. This is particularly necessary given the manner in which teachers in public schools are consistently subject to administrative dictates and school conditions that undermine their power and authority. As teachers struggle together to challenge their conflicts and contradictions in this area, they are more able to build environments that support an emancipatory view of authority, stimulating their students to rethink critically their values, ideas, and actions in relation to the consequences these might have on themselves and others.

Although the question of authority is seldom discussed in liberatory terms by either conservative or liberal educators, it is essential that it be critically addressed in teacher preparation programs. As mentioned above, it is difficult for teachers to address the issue of authority if they themselves hold uncritical, conflicting, and contradictory attitudes about power and its relationship to human organization. Such attitudes are apparent in prevailing commonsense beliefs about the nature of power. While conservative educators are more likely to see power as a positive force that works to maintain order, earn respect, and "get the job done," liberals—and even many radical educators—are more prone to believe that "power corrupts" and that, despite human efforts, power ultimately leads to destruction. As a consequence, power is commonly perceived either as an absolute force for good, or else as an evil or negative force that dehumanizes and divests the individual's capacity for justice and solidarity with others. Understanding how these views of power are enmeshed in the contradictory thinking of teachers can help to shed light on the inadequacy and helplessness that so many educators express. This is of particular concern, given the fact that so many liberal and radical educators who hold negative assumptions related to power also speak to the necessity of *empowering* students, communities, and teachers alike.

The contradictory assumptions that underscore the question of authority also function to perpetuate the status quo, through the manner in which they sabotage, limit, and distort teachers' perceptions of classroom authority and their ability to alter the conditions they find in public schools. Such teachers, who do not possess a dialectical view of authority, generally lack the critical criteria to challenge attitudes, beliefs, and actions that perpetuate social injustice. In light of this, authority can be more readily understood in terms of its potential to uphold those emancipatory categories essential to the foundation of critical democratic life.

In our efforts to address this dimension, it must be explained that contradictory assumptions of authority cannot be deconstructed by simply utilizing a language of practice. The task of challenging society's contradictions requires educators to delve fearlessly into both the abstract and concrete experiences that unite to inform the theoretical realm. Through uniting their critical reflections of practice with theory, teachers come to discover the manner in which distorted views of power inform those classroom practices that reinforce undercurrents of oppression, perpetuating conditions that marginalize and alienate students of color.

The authoritarian nature of a conservative view of teacher authority is often hidden beneath the guise of traditional notions of respect, which can incorporate objective, instrumental, and hierarchical relationships that support various forms of oppressive educational practices at the expense of student voice. On the other hand, the oppressive impact of the liberal view of teacher authority, which all but disengages with questions of authority, often functions in an equally perverse manner. Hidden under the values of subjectivity, individualism, and intentionality, this view easily deteriorates into a crass relativism, asserting that all expressed values and ideas are deserving of equal time (Giroux, 1981). This is put into practice to the extent that some teachers proudly proclaim that they always consider all ideas generated by their students as equal, irrespective of personal histories, ideologies, or cultural differences—thus professing a specious notion of shared power. Although this perspective may ring true when entertained exclusively in the language of practice, theoretically it reflects an uncritical disengagement with issues related to social forms of domination and the manner in which ideas are generated and informed by particular interest that silence and oppress students from subordinate groups. Therefore, it is fraudulent to pretend that a teacher does not possess the authority and power over students to determine how the classroom will be governed; and it is an act of irresponsibility for teachers to abdicate their duty to challenge critically the oppressive nature of student ideas when these ideas constitute acts of racism, sexism, classism, or other forms of psychological violence that attack the dignity and self-worth of students of color.

Unlike traditional views on teacher authority, an emancipatory view of authority suggests that, although teachers hold knowledge that is considered to render them prepared to enter the classroom, they must come to recognize that knowledge as a historical and cultural product is forever in a creative state of partiality. And, as a consequence, all forms of discourse represent only one small piece of the larger puzzle that constitutes all possible knowledge at any given moment in time. Hence, all forms of knowledge must be open for question, examination, and critique by and with students in the process of learning. In this way, teachers actively use their authority to create the conditions for a critical transformation of consciousness that takes place in the process of the interaction of teacher, students, and the knowledge they produce together. Grounded in criteria informed by a liberatory vision of life, teachers embrace the notion of authority in the interest of cultural democracy, rather than against it.

REDEFINING FAIRNESS AND EQUALITY

If American public schools are to establish classroom environments that are culturally democratic, teachers will have to undertake a critical analysis of what has been traditionally defined as *fair and equal*. Just as the principles of democracy have so often been reduced to numerical head-counts and majority rule, concepts of fairness and equality have also been reduced to such quantifiable forms. Therefore, it is not unusual to hear teachers across the country express the belief that fair-and-equal is equivalent to providing the same quantity and quality of goods to all students across the board, irrespective of differences in social privilege and economic entitlement.

Clearly inherent in this perspective of fair-and-equal is the elimination of any transformative impact that these principles might have on the lives of disenfranchised students. The consequence in public schools is that students from the dominant culture who enter with major social and economic advantages receive as much—and at times even more—than students from subordinate cultures who arrive with far fewer social advantages. In an analysis of resource distribution among students in public schools, it is unquestionably apparent that poor children, who receive the least at home, receive the least from public education (Kozol, 1990). This painfully reminds us that the American educational system has little to do with cultivating equality. For if equality was, in fact, a part of the philosophical vision of education, the educational system would prioritize its resources in such a manner as to ensure that the majority of students were placed in settings where they could achieve successfully. Under such conditions, students from disenfranchised communities who require more educational opportunities by way of teacher contact, educational materials, nutritional support, and health care would receive more, while those students who arrive with greater privileges and with many more resources already in place would receive less.

Instead, what we find in most schools is the opposite. Students from the dominant culture who excel because they have been raised in homes that can provide them with the social, economic, and cultural capital necessary to meet the elitist and ethnocentric standards of American schools enjoy greater advantages and more positive regard than those from disenfranchised communities who must consistently struggle to succeed under social conditions working to their detriment. For decades it has been well documented that students from the dominant culture, who are raised in environments of privilege, score higher on standardized examinations. Hence, these students are perceived as superior when compared to most bicultural students. In addition, many of these superior students are also considered by public schools to be exhibiting mentally gifted abilities, while the majority of students of color are stigmatized and shamed by assignments into basic and remedial classes. This mentally gifted status has then been used as a justifiable rationale for appropriating additional resources to the already privileged—a group that just happens to include very few working-class students of color.

The consequence here is that the majority of bicultural students who are in need of greater school resources and educational opportunities find themselves in less challenging and less stimulating environments—environments that operate under the assumption that the students themselves, their parents, and their culture are to blame for their deficiency, while ignoring the deficiencies of a larger social caste system that replicates itself in public schools. Efforts by the White House in the past decade have merely functioned to make the situation worse. Plans that had been made to equalize school funding among districts have been replaced by a major reduction of funding to educational programs and an emphasis on building student motivation and self-control. Jonathan Kozol suggests that the consequences of tougher conservative rhetoric and more severe demands have led to further discrimination toward disenfranchised students:

Higher standards, in the absence of authentic educative opportunities in early years, function as a punitive attack on those who have been cheated since their infancy. Effectively, we now ask more of those to whom we now give less. Earlier testing for schoolchildren is prescribed. Those who fail are penalized by being held back from promotion and by being slotted into lower tracks where they cannot impede the progress of more privileged children. Those who disrupt classroom discipline are not placed in smaller classes with more patient teachers; instead, at a certain point, they are expelled—even if this means expulsion of a quarter of all pupils in school. (Kozol, 1990, p. 52)

Buried deep within traditional institutional views of fairness and equality is a stubborn refusal to engage with the reality of social conditions that marginalize students of color in this country. As a consequence, not only are bicultural students perceived as somehow less intelligent and therefore less deserving than middle-class students from the dominant culture, but also they are taught through their interactions with the system to perceive themselves in this way. If conditions in public schools are to change, teachers must openly challenge traditional views of fairness and equality and expose how these have functioned to reinforce notions of entitlement and privilege based on a doctrine of Social Darwinism that has proven to be incompatible with any emancipatory vision of social justice and equality.

THE USE OF MULTICULTURAL CURRICULUM

When educators first begin to think about how they can meet the needs of students of color, one of the most common places to begin is by bringing traditional cultural objects and symbols into the classroom. In fact, most multicultural curricula place a major emphasis on such cultural artifacts because they can be easily seen, manipulated, and quantified, although they ignore the more complex subjectivities of cultural values, belief systems, and traditions that inform the production of such cultural forms. Also problematic are depictions of cultural images and symbols that promote Eurocentric interpretations of cultural groups—depictions that function to dissolve cultural differences and reinforce mainstream expectations of assimilation. As a consequence, these traditional multicultural approaches operate to the detriment of students of color because they fail to respect and affirm their cultural differences and to help them understand the social and political implications of growing up bicultural in American society.

This is not to imply that bicultural students should not be exposed to curriculum that seeks to present cultural artifacts affirming their cultural traditions and experiences, but rather to emphasize that such multicultural materials and activities do not, in and of themselves, ensure that a culturally democratic process is at work. As mentioned above, this is in fact the case with most traditional efforts to promote cultural diversity. And many situations exist in which students are presented with games, food, stories, language, music, and other cultural forms in such a way as to strip these expressions of intent by reducing them to mere objects disembodied from their cultural meaning.

In order to prevent such an outcome, educators must become more critical not only of the actual curriculum they bring into the classroom, but also of the philosophical beliefs that inform their practice. First, they can begin to assess carefully their personal assumptions, prejudices, and biases related to issues of culture. Since it is far more common for teachers to think of themselves as neutral and unbiased toward all students, many racist, classist, and sexist attitudes and behaviors are most often disguised by faulty common-sense assumptions utilized extensively to assess student academic performance or classroom behavior. For example, most teachers still retain notions of culture that reflect color-blind or melting-pot assumptions and a bootstrap mentality. Simply put, these teachers believe that all people are the same in spite of race or culture, that the United States is a place where all cultures have (or should have) melted together to form one culture, and that anyone who wants to succeed *can* succeed, irrespective of social or economic circumstances.

Unfortunately these assumptions work to undermine the emancipatory potential of multicultural curricula. This is primarily because, when educators engage with issues related to cultural diversity based on these beliefs, they are unable accurately to address cultural issues related to power and dominance, as well as the impact that these forces have on the lives of bicultural students. For instance, in situations where students of color act out their resistance to cultural domination by passively refusing to participate in classroom activities or by actively disrupting the process, these student behaviors are interpreted by the majority of teachers as simply a classroom management problem—or, at most, as cause for concern about the emotional stability or well-being of the student. Seldom does it occur to most teachers who are faced with such behaviors to consider the manner in which cultural subordination and prevailing social hostility toward differences might represent the genesis of classroom resistance. Consequently, despite well-meaning efforts by teachers to intervene, their faulty assumptions generally hinder their effectiveness with bicultural students through unintentional acts of cultural invasion and further cultural subordination of students of color.

Second, in order to approach effectively the need for culturally relevant curriculum in the classroom, educators must be willing to acknowledge their limitations with respect to the cultural systems from which bicultural students make sense of their world. This requires teachers to recognize that students and their families bring to the classroom knowledge about their cultures, their communities, and their educational needs. This can best be accomplished by creating conditions for students to voice more clearly what constitutes the cultural differences they experience and to unfurl the conflicts as they struggle together to understand their own histories and their relationships with others. In addition, teachers must take the time to learn about the communities in which their students live. As teachers gain a greater understanding of students' lives outside of school, they are more able to create opportunities for classroom dialogue, which assists bicultural students to affirm, challenge, and transform the many conflicts and contradictions that they face as members of an oppressed group.

Third, educators also need to become more critical in their assessment of multicultural curricula and activities with respect to the consequences of their use in the classroom. For example, many teachers believe that making feathered headbands and teaching students about the Indians' contributions to the first Thanksgiving are effective activities for the study of Native Americans. In reality, these types of activities constitute forms of cultural invasion that reinforce stereotypical images of American Indians and grossly distort the history of a people. Although this is a deeply problematic representation of culture for all students, it has a particularly perverse effect on students who have had little or no exposure to Native Americans other than what they have seen on television and in films, and a destructive impact on the self-esteem and identity of Native American students who are victimized by such distorted depictions of their cultural histories.

And fourth, teachers must come to realize that no multicultural curriculum, in and of itself, can replace the dialogical participation of bicultural students in the process of schooling. This is to say that even the most ideologically correct curriculum is in danger of objectifying students if it is utilized in such a way as to detach them from their everyday lives. Gramsci (1971) observes, "Thus, we come back to the truly active participation of the pupil in the school, which can only exist if the school is related to life. The more the new curricula nominally affirm and theorize the pupil's activity and working collaboration with the teacher, the more they are actually designed as if the pupil were purely passive" (p. 37).

Gramsci's words support the notion that a genuine affirmation of cultural diversity in the classroom requires the restructuring of power relations and classroom structures in such a manner as to promote the *active* voice and participation of bicultural students. Through the creation of culturally democratic classroom conditions that also place bicultural voices at the center of the discourse, all students can come together to speak out about their lives and engage in dialogues that permit them to examine their cultural values and social realities. In this way, students can learn to make problematic their views of life, search for different ways to think about themselves, challenge their self-imposed as well as institutionally defined limitations, affirm their cultural and individual strengths, and embrace the possibilities for a better world through a growing sense of solidarity built on love, respect, and compassion for one another and a commitment to the liberation of all people.

CHALLENGING RACISM IN THE CLASSROOM

No matter how much a teacher might feel committed to the notion of cultural diversity, it is impossible to create a culturally democratic environment that can effectively meet the educational needs of bicultural students if that teacher is ill equipped to challenge incidences of racism when they surface in the curriculum or in student relationships. As described earlier, racism results from institutionalized prejudices and biases that perpetuate discrimination based on racial and cultural differences. When educators fail to criticize discriminatory attitudes and behaviors, they permit bicultural students to suffer needless humiliation and psychological violence that negatively reinforce feelings of disentitlement and marginalization in society.

Despite attitudes to the contrary, cultural differences do not constitute the problem in public schools; rather, the problem is directly related to the responses of the dominant culture to these differences—responses that function to perpetuate social, political, and economic inequality. Instead of adopting the neutral position of most multicultural approaches, Carol Phillips suggests that educators teach students how to recognize when cultural and racially different groups are being victimized by the racist and biased attitudes of the larger society; how these behaviors are institutionalized in the policies and procedures of [schools] and programs; how these practices of excluding people are so mystified that well-meaning advocates for change fail to see them operating; [and] how to act against prevailing forces that perpetuate racism. (Phillips, 1988, p. 45)

The inability to address racism, as suggested by Phillips, is commonly observed in the failure of educators to address even racial slurs when they occur. A common scenario may find two or more students in a disagreement, and one or more may yell out at the other, "You nigger!" or "You greaser!" More times than not, educators who overhear such comments—unable to deal with their own discomfort—let them go by altogether, or they may tell the students to stop fighting, or that it is against the rules to call each other names. Unfortunately, despite good intentions, these approaches ignore the social circumstances that inform such behavior and the consequences for all students involved. In addition, it does nothing to assist these students and their peers to understand their actions critically, nor will it transform their relationships in any way.

Educators who strive for culturally democratic environments will need to call on their courage and inner strength to challenge the tension and discomfort they experience when confronting issues of discrimination in the classroom. Instead of looking for quick-fix methods to restore a false sense of harmony at such moments of confrontation, educators must seek to unveil the tensions, conflicts, and contradictions that perpetuate discriminatory attitudes and behaviors among their students. In a situation such as the one described above, the teacher can bring students together into a critical dialogue about racial epithets and their role in perpetuating injustice. This may begin with questions about the feelings that precipitate these words: Where did they learn the words? What is the intent behind their use? What are the effects of these epithets on the victim? On the victimizer? How does this behavior relate to other forms of racism in the community? How could students engage in resolving their differences in other ways?

Dialogues such as this should be consistently introduced and encouraged among students within the context of the classroom, so that they may come to understand how their attitudes and behaviors affect others and, more importantly, so that they may come to act in behalf of all who are oppressed. Through their participation in this process, students have the opportunity to speak their feelings about race and how it relates to their lived experiences, and to become conscious of their own investment in racist attitudes and behaviors. In addition, they also learn to analyze how racism affects the conditions that exist in their communities, and to develop strategies for countering racism when they encounter it in their own lives (Giroux, 1990). For bicultural students, the dialogue must extend further. It must also assist them to identify the different ways in which their relationships with the dominant culture have conditioned them to take on contradictory attitudes and beliefs about themselves that cause them to participate unintentionally in the perpetuation of their own oppression.

THE CULTURE OF THE TEACHER

Whenever educators begin seriously to confront the complexity of teaching in bicultural communities, they also begin to question what impact the teacher's cultural background has on her or his ability to educate successfully students of color. It is an important question to consider within the context of a critical bicultural pedagogical discourse—particularly because of the profound nature of cultural belief systems and their relationship to issues of identity and social power. In addition, it brings into the arena of discussion notions of cultural differences with respect to the roles that teachers play if they are from the dominant culture, versus those who come from subordinate cultures.

As suggested earlier, in their efforts to learn about different cultural communities, teachers generally pursue materials that address the more visible or tangible aspects of cultural experience, while neglecting the deep structural values that inform the cultural worldviews of subordinate groups. In conjunction with this, teachers have been socialized to believe that by simply gathering or obtaining information on any particular subject they can come to know. From a critical bicultural perspective, learning about a culture from a book or a few seminars does not constitute knowing that culture. This is particularly true with respect to understanding the daily lived experiences of the group and the historicity of social forces that work to shape and shift how its members interact in the world. For example, someone who is not Hopi might read many books or articles about the Hopi people and yet still not know what it means to grow up as a Hopi in American society.

To even begin to comprehend the bicultural experience requires that teachers from the dominant culture invest time and energy into establishing critical dialogues with people of color if they wish to understand their communities better. Even then, these teachers must recognize and respect that their process of learning and knowing is inherently situated *outside* that cultural context, and is therefore different from the knowledge obtained from living *within* a particular cultural community. This is an essential understanding for teachers who have been raised in the dominant culture and whose cultural reference point is based on White Euroamerican values—which are the predominant values informing most American institutions. This is not to say that all Anglo-Americans conform to these values, but rather to suggest that, even in states of nonconformity, Euroamerican values represent the central reference point that individuals of the dominant culture move toward or move away from in the course of their personal and institutional relationships. This reference point also dictates the multitude of subject positions that individuals from the dominant culture assume in their lives with respect to class, gender, sexual orientation, spirituality, politics, and other ideological categories related to worldview.

The biculturation process discussed in Chapter 3 represents an attempt to describe the dynamics by which people of color interact with the conflicts and contradictions arising when growing up in a primary culture that dictates a reference point and subject positions in conflict with those of the dominant culture. As a consequence, members from subordinate groups must find ways to cope and function within institutional environments that on the one hand generally undermine and curtail their rights to equality, and on the other hand push them to assimilate the values of the dominant culture. The different ways in which bicultural people attempt to resolve the tension created by such forces are reflected in the predominant response patterns they utilize to survive. What complicates this process further is the manner in which Euroamerican values are perpetuated through hegemonic forces of social control, while the primary values of African-Americans, Latinos, Native Americans, Asians, and other subordinate groups are relegated to subordinate positions in American society.

The consequence is that very often people of color whose bicultural voices and experiences have been systematically silenced and negated are not necessarily conscious of the manner in which racism and classism have influenced their individual development, nor how they have functioned to distort perceptions of their cultural group within an Anglocentric world. Therefore, the fact that a person is bicultural does not guarantee that she or he occupies a position of resistance to such domination. In fact, under current social conditions, it is not unusual to find people of color in positions of power who ignore issues of social power and perpetuate ideas and beliefs that function to the detriment of their own people. Such prominent figures include the likes of Senator Samuel Hayakawa, who was an outspoken advocate for a national English-only initiative; Linda Chavez, a former member of the National Human Relations Commission; and Shelby Steele, the author of *The Content of Our Character*. This is also the case with the many teachers of color who have naively made attempts to assimilate into the dominant culture without critically engaging with the impact of their beliefs on their lives and work.

This perspective is offered here because it represents a reality that must be understood if educators are honestly to consider questions related to the cultural background of the teachers who educate bicultural students. It is a reality that must be acknowledged if we are to prevent falling into the trap of essentialist arguments, such as those proclaiming that only teachers of color can effectively educate students of color. Instead, what is needed is the courage, willingness, and desire to speak honestly to those issues that relate directly to how individuals define their cultural identity and how this influences their work with bicultural students. How teachers perceive the notion of cultural identity is especially important, given that the majority of educators in the United States are members of the dominant culture, and that most educators—of all cultures—have been schooled in traditional pedagogical models. Hence, the teacher's cultural background, espoused ideology, and academic preparation embody equally important areas of concern in our efforts to create conditions that are conducive to a culturally democratic life in the classroom.

If public schools are to provide successfully for the educational needs of bicultural students, they must work in collaboration with bicultural educators, students, parents, and their communities. Anything short of this effort suggests an educational process that is in danger of oppressing and disempowering students of color. This is not to imply that all teachers in bicultural communities must necessarily be teachers of color, but rather to emphasize that it is an arrogant and patronizing gesture for educators from the dominant culture to think that they can meet the needs of a culturally different community when they fail to work in solidarity with educators and other members of that community.

Efforts to establish solidarity among culturally diverse groups require relationships based on mutual respect and equality. White teachers need to abandon, willingly, unfair notions of entitlement and privilege so they may enter into relationships with people of color that support the struggle for freedom and a better world. This requires that White educators acknowledge the manner in which people of color have been historically discriminated against and subordinated to inferior positions in the society at large and the manner in which public education has perpetuated this process. They must come to see how these injustices actually exist in their own profession by the very nature of the assumptions that inform their practice. For example, it is not unusual to find bicultural/bilingual instructional aides with ten or more years of experience in the classroom working under inexperienced White middle-class teachers who know very little about the actual needs of bicultural students. Yet, when such conditions are challenged as part of a wider struggle for more bilingual/bicultural teachers, it is interesting to note the manner in which questions of social control ultimately inform the responses of many public school districts. Rather than create the conditions for well-experienced instructional aides to complete their education and receive certification, many large urban school districts have decided to import teachers from Spain. These are teachers who, in fact, are less knowledgeable of the American bicultural experience than Euroamerican educators. This illustrates only one of the ways in which a process of hegemony operates in public schools to sabotage the transformative struggles of oppressed communities and to ensure the perpetuation of the status quo. Such forms of hegemony can be understood by teachers and challenged in the course of their work.

Further, in order for bicultural students to develop both an individual and social sense of empowerment in their lives, they need to establish relationships with both White and bicultural teachers who are genuinely committed to a democratic vision of community life. When students actually experience the process of White teachers and bicultural teachers working together to address issues related to cultural differences and conflicts, they also come to better understand cultural democracy and learn to participate in cross-cultural dialogues in ways that truly respect and honor the emancipatory rights of all people.

Critical educators from the dominant culture demonstrate a spirit of solidarity and possibility when they willingly challenge both cultural values and institutional conditions of inequity despite the fact that these potentially function to their material benefit. Their refusal to accept social conditions of entitlement and privilege for themselves at the expense of oppressed groups helps to lay the groundwork for relations with people of color based on a solidarity and commitment to social justice and equality. Such educators truly recognize the need to create conditions in the classroom that empower students of color and to open opportunities that historically have remained closed to these students. Operating from this perspective, programs developed under such mandates as affirmative action and equal educational opportunity are given support as beginning efforts toward social equality, rather than seen as somehow taking away from members of the dominant culture. The way in which teachers themselves address these issues in the larger world is significant, because it usually also reflects how they relate with students of color in the course of their daily interactions with them in the classroom.

It is also essential that students of color experience a variety of teachers of color during the course of their schooling. Bicultural educators who are socially conscious bring a wealth of knowledge and experience that often resonates with the realities that students of color experience in their own lives. Many of these teachers are bilingual, understand the complexity of their students' cultural worldviews, are knowledgeable about their history and literature, are cognizant of the different styles in which students learn and communicate, are conscious of the rules of appropriate relationships and interactions among people, and know the communities from which their students come. As a consequence, bicultural teachers are generally more able to use their own learning experiences and knowledge of their cultural values to develop effective curricula that engage with issues related to cultural diversity. In addition, through their knowledge of community, they are able to find ways in which to integrate the students' lived culture into classroom relationships. They are also more genuinely able to affirm and support the development of the bicultural voice, given their ability to engage with the lived conditions of cultural domination and resistance. Hence, it must be recognized that bicultural teachers serve vital roles as models for students of color—many of whom have seldom witnessed people of color in positions of power and influence. Most importantly, through their experiences with critical bicultural educators, bicultural students are more concretely challenged and supported as they come to redefine their possiblities within the context of American society.

RESTRUCTURING PUBLIC SCHOOLS

Critical educators of bicultural students must consider creative ways in which they can work to restructure public school environments that support experiences of culturally democratic life. The manner in which this is done must take into account not only the specific needs that bicultural students bring into the classroom, but also the needs that teachers have in order to be more effective educators. Through gaining a better understanding of the lived histories and daily lives of both students of color and their teachers, classroom structures can be transformed to reflect meaningful social relationships and critical pedagogical approaches that are built on the principles of cultural democracy. Just as students are critically challenged to redefine the possibilities for transforming the world, their teachers should be actively involved in such a process within the context of their own profession.

First of all, efforts by teachers to promote the development of voice, participation, social responsibility, and solidarity are strongly reflected in the way they physically structure and situate the learning environment in their classrooms. A few classroom changes that would address this concern include these examples:

Cambios en el Salón

- The furniture, and in particular the seating in the room, is arranged so as to permit free physical movement of students about the classroom.

- Classroom spaces promote working in groups and on collaborative projects.

- Classroom bulletin boards are generated in conjunction with the participation of students, who are encouraged to utilize materials that are meaningful to them. These forms of cultural expression are then used to stimulate dialogues about their relationship to the context of students' lives and communities.

- Curricular activities are created for students to have opportunities to converse in their home languages with each other and to introduce various aspects of their language experience to other students.

- Students are actively involved in the development of classroom rules and in making decisions about classroom activities whenever possible. In addition, they are involved in dialogues designed to help them consider the consequences of rules and decisions made with respect to themselves as individuals and the class as a whole.

It is important to note that none of these suggestions, in and of itself, constitutes *the* way to incorporate a critical bicultural pedagogy, for the manner in which a critical pedagogy evolves in any particular classroom environment must be based on the contextual conditions present. No lesson plan or curriculum should ever supersede the actual learning needs expressed by students or identified by the teacher. Learning is a contextual experience by which knowledge and meaning are produced within the complexity of a multitude of potential responses generated by students and teacher alike.

The few suggestions mentioned above focus on what teachers can do to transform the structures and relationships within their own classrooms. But outside the classroom, there is also much to be done related to the general restructuring of the working conditions that teachers find in public schools. Critical educators must explore some possible ways in which to transform these conditions so that schools may function to support their own empowerment as well as an emancipatory vision for education. Some suggestions to consider with respect to this concern are as follows:

- The development of cross-cultural teaching teams in schools with large bicultural student populations.

- The initiation of professional development opportunities for all teachers to become knowledgeable in the principles of a critical bicultural pedagogy. This would provide teachers the opportunity to better understand the bicultural experience of students and to examine together their own prejudices and biases related to issues of cultural diversity.

- A greater involvement of teachers in the development, evaluation, and selection of texts, films, and other instructional materials.

- An ongoing collaborative effort with parents and community members to transform the educational environments of public schools.

- Establishment of regular public forums within schools to discuss issues related to bicultural students, such as bilingualism, the bicultural process, the academic needs of students, parent involvement in the classroom, and so forth.

In addition, teachers must also struggle to transform the structural conditions related to both out-of-class work and class size. Much of the demoralization teachers experience is not, for the most part, a consequence of low pay; rather, it is more closely linked to the powerlessness generated by working in an environment that is fundamentally incompatible with engaging in the complexities of teaching a culturally diverse student population. In order to address this issue, public school teachers might begin by demanding that the number of students in their classrooms be limited to approximately twenty. It is not unusual to find public schools in large urban settings where teachers are assigned up to forty students, with limited assistance from an instructional aide. One of the most revolutionary actions that public school teachers can take, at this point in time, is to assume an uncompromising posture with respect to the issue of class size. It is well documented that students are more successful when they receive more individualized attention from the teacher. So completely conscious of this fact are private schools that they use as a major selling point their policy of small class size. Teacher unions and other teacher organizations need to become advocates for themselves as well as for disenfranchised students by asserting the entitlement of the latter to the rights enjoyed by students from privileged classes. Most importantly, teachers who are less burdened by the tremendous demands placed on them by large class size are more able to engage consistently and critically with the actual needs of bicultural students and issues related to cultural diversity.

Also of major importance is the struggle for the redefinition of the teacher's workday. Seldom are teachers afforded opportunities to come together on an ongoing basis to reflect and dialogue critically about the concerns they experience in their efforts to meet the needs of their students. And even more seldom do they have the time to maintain some consistent form of personal contact with parents, despite the fact that studies clearly indicate this to be a significant factor in the achievement of bicultural students (Rashid, 1981; Goldenberg, 1987; Cummins, 1986). Teachers require institutional support in their efforts to develop working relationships with their colleagues, students, parents, and the communities in which they work. This can only take place when the teacher's work is redefined more realistically to include both what teachers are required to implement daily in their classrooms and those important functions they must perform outside the classroom setting to be effective educators. But this redefinition can only take place when teachers struggle to transform the conditions of their labor within the context of a critical process that is generated by working together for a better life—not only as educators, but as workers and free democratic citizens.

BEYOND DESPAIR

Much frustration is evident in the attitudes and responses of many educators to the conditions they find in public schools. Many teachers blame the problems they experience on the increasing number of students of color. Others are acutely aware that they were insufficiently prepared by teacher education programs to meet the needs of a culturally diverse student population. Still others experience a deep feeling of personal frustration, which they attribute to their own individual failure as teachers. Whatever the manner in which teachers define the cause of their frustration, it is clear that their perceptions echo a great sense of despair and powerlessness.

It is important to note that those teachers who find themselves within public school conditions—where their voices are silenced and their opportunities to decide on curricula, texts, and other classroom requirements are limited—are most in danger of experiencing a sense of despair. Public school teachers in these environments must work together to challenge themselves and each other to move beyond the limitations that they find in these schools. In addition, they must also move beyond their own dependency on traditional classroom structures and the artifacts that support the perpetuation of their disempowerment.

For example, under such conditions as described above, teachers must initially cultivate their creative abilities to utilize commonplace materials and natural environments that can serve as ideal conditions for students to investigate the ordinary, and through acting on it discover their potential power to create and change their world. Given this approach, any classroom situation can potentially be converted into a critical environment as educators discover the multitude of pedagogical possibilities at their disposal. But this can only take place when educators courageously abandon old and disempowering notions of what is necessary and certain, and move beyond the boundaries of prescribed educational practice and into the realm of creativity and discovery.

As emphasized earlier, fundamental to creating the conditions for cultural democracy is a political commitment to a liberatory vision. A critical bicultural pedagogy can only emerge within a social context where teachers are grounded in a commitment to both individual and social empowerment. Hence, the smaller political endeavor of the classroom is not seen as simply an encapsulated moment in time, but rather it is consistently connected to a greater democratic political project. From this vantage point, teachers function as empowered social agents of history, who are firmly committed to collaborative struggles for transformation as they seek to change and redefine the conditions that threaten the opportunities for voice, participation, and solidarity in their schools. As teachers work in solidarity with their colleagues, parents, students, and the community, they discover their tremendous collective power, and through this process of affirmation move beyond despair. It is, in part, this critical commitment to act in behalf of freedom and social justice that also serves as a model for their students to discover their own personal power, social transformative potential, and spirit of hope.

Embodied in this emancipatory spirit of hope is also a faith in the capacity of human beings to transform the oppressive and dehumanizing conditions that disconnect, fragment, and alienate us from one another. Grounded in this struggle by a collective vision of liberation, critical educators search out creative ways to expand the opportunities for students of color to become authentic beings for themselves, in spite of the limitations of traditional curricula and prevailing social conditions. Students are encouraged to question the conflicts, contradictions, disjunctions, and partiality of standardized knowledge forms—in their own lives as well. Consistently, liberatory educators support and challenge bicultural students to struggle together so that they may come to know all the possibilities that might be available to them as free citizens. For it is through this critical process of discovery and empowerment that teachers and students move in solidarity across the terrain of cultural differences to arrive at the knowledge that hidden in the complexity of these differences are many ways to be human, and many ways to struggle for a world in which we can all be free.

CHAPTER 6

INFORMING PRACTICE: THE PACIFIC OAKS COLLEGE BICULTURAL DEVELOPMENT PROGRAM

> Our work here has shown me that although we may be different,
> by working together we can find our common ground and work
> to make this world a better place for all people.
>
> Excerpt from a student evaluation,
> Pacific Oaks College, 1988

The primary purpose of this last chapter is to discuss the Bicultural Development Program at Pacific Oaks College. This program illustrates an effort to incorporate the bicultural education theory discussed in this book into the design of a teacher education program specifically focused on preparing educators to meet effectively the pedagogical needs of bicultural students. This discussion will include some background on the college itself, a description of the program and its requirements, the student evaluation process, and an example of how a critical bicultural pedagogy functions within the context of the classroom.

PACIFIC OAKS COLLEGE

Pacific Oaks was founded as a nursery school and community education center in 1945 by seven Quaker families. The teacher education program of Pacific Oaks grew out of the need to train teachers for the nursery school. Over the years, the center expanded and the college was established. Pacific Oaks is now a children's school and fully accredited college. The college offers upper division and graduate programs in human development and preparation for teaching credentials. In addition to teachers, the programs serve individuals working in the helping professions, including counseling, nursing, and other human service fields. The college serves approximately 500 students, on campus and through its outreach programs.

The Pacific Oaks philosophy would most appropriately be defined as humanistic, developmental, and universal in nature. Three basic concepts underlie the college's philosophy: (1) that growth is a dynamic and lifelong process; (2) that every individual has a fundamental worth; and (3) that each person, no matter how young or old, has a unique identity and human potential that she or he contributes to the lives of all those with whom she or he comes in contact. Experiential learning—that is, learning by doing—is at the heart of the curriculum for adults, as it is for the children enrolled in the children's school. The college espouses the notion that both theory and practice are learned through action and interaction, and students are encouraged to value their practice as well as the theoretical aspects of their learning. Consequently, all programs at the college include a fieldwork, or practicum, component that requires students to participate in an educational setting where they gain hands-on experience working with children and adults.

The Mission Statement

Pacific Oaks is an independent institution of learning influenced by its Quaker heritage and dedicated to the principles of social justice, respect for diversity, and the valuing of the uniqueness of each person. Its primary focus is placed upon all needs of young children and their families, and all those who, in a direct or indirect manner, touch their lives each day. Education at Pacific Oaks includes academic, research, clinical, and community outreach components to develop an understanding of those settings within which a child acts and which, in turn affect a child's development. Pacific Oaks promotes educational practices within the institution, profession, and public schools that encourage learners to find their voice, to take stands in the face of opposition, and to exercise competence in collaboration with others.

The Pacific Oaks mission statement, written essentially by the faculty and approved by the board of trustees in 1986, reflects a liberal commitment to the individual and a concern for issues of diversity and social change. Yet, despite a stated philosophical commitment to "social justice, respect for diversity, and the valuing of the uniqueness of each person," the college has always struggled in carrying out this commitment in practice, and the major reason for this phenomenon is related to the institutional contradictions that arise as a result of economics and the dominant cultural ideology.

A basic issue in terms of economics has to do with the college's extreme dependency on student tuition and private contributions for its survival. This economic dependency plays an essential role in limiting the number of students of color the college can serve. The majority of potential bicultural students can only attend if they receive financial aid from the institution. The declining number of available scholarships, fellowships, and loans functions to reduce the cultural diversity among the student population.

Issues related to cultural ideology and student diversity are often sensitive and volatile, and thus difficult to identify and confront. The issues that Pacific Oaks must face are closely related to the earlier discussion on the liberal educational discourse and its shortcomings with respect to students of color. Unfortunately, the college's instructors, who for the most part espouse a liberal discourse, often fall into the trap of victim-blaming and accept relativistic notions of knowledge that are clearly fueled by their views of childhood determinism, universalism, and a heavy emphasis on individual subjectivity. Consequently, despite their consistently expressed vision of pluralism, the faculty and administration often fail to recognize the fundamental inequities inherent in an institutional structure that is supported by interests that do not, for the most part, benefit working-class people or students of color.

These contradictions are acted out, directly or indirectly, in the classroom—functioning to alienate (unwittingly) bicultural students, and to reduce their opportunities to build their critical abilities and develop their bicultural voice. When bicultural students resist (consciously or unconsciously) the oppression that ensues, the faculty is seldom prepared to contend with the needs of these students. Hence, although Pacific Oaks represents a liberal alternative school, it continues to struggle with some of the very same problems related to diversity found in other, more traditional teacher education programs across the country. It is important to note that, in spite of these contradictions, Pacific Oaks—as educator and advocate—has always held fast to a commitment to the healthy development of children.

During the past ten years, as a result of the work done by a core group of radical teachers at the college to confront these contradictions, the trustees, administration, and other faculty members have been unable to ignore their institutional commitment to the issue of diversity. Consequently, this struggle has been responsible for the hiring of more faculty of color, the development of an antibias curriculum for young children, the institutionalization of a requirement that all students take a course focusing specifically on the impact of race, class, culture, and gender on development, and the establishment of the Bicultural Development Program.

THE BICULTURAL DEVELOPMENT PROGRAM

The Bicultural Development Program has been developed specifically in response to the rapidly growing concerns over the high dropout rate of bicultural students in major urban cities. The statistics are particularly alarming, in light of the demographic predictions currently being made by social scientists in the field who project that by the year 2000 many states in the nation will be composed of primarily bicultural populations. That is to say, the majority of these states will have residents who are born into families whose primary culture differs from the mainstream dominant culture.

This constitutes a major concern for American education, since most of today's educational settings do not have a sufficient number of teachers and administrators who are prepared to meet the changing needs of an expanding bicultural student enrollment. Daily we see the gap widening between the traditional teacher preparation received by the majority of educators and the pedagogical requirements for effectively educating bicultural students. It is precisely this gap that the Bicultural Development

Program is designed to bridge. In many ways, the program represents an innovative and concerted effort to meet the urgent need for educators who can critically engage with a world that is swiftly changing.

This is particularly significant, given the intense morale problems and the consequent premature exiting of a great number of teachers from the public schools. Rather than blaming teachers for abandoning their commitment to public education, it is important to examine traditional teacher education programs for what they fail to provide. Specifically, these programs have failed to prepare teachers to contend critically with the particular needs of the culturally diverse student populations found in most large cities. Instead, they "train" teachers in a technocratic and instrumental banking system of education that ignores altogether the relationship of pedagogy, politics, and culture.

The Bicultural Development Program, on the other hand, incorporates these categories at the core of its theory and practice. With this in mind, the program argues that teachers who are committed to cultural democracy, understand bicultural development, are knowledgeable about critical pedagogy, and are engaged in an ongoing analysis of their own values, experiences, fears, concerns, biases, and prejudices—both in theory and in practice— are most able to contend with the realities they must face in bicultural classrooms. Further, it is quite evident that when teachers feel they are effective in their classrooms they will actually experience fewer problems related to morale, and consequently suffer a lower rate of burnout than teachers who feel inadequately prepared to meet the needs of their students.

The Bicultural Development Program is geared for teachers, administrators, and others who are, or will be, working in predominantly bicultural communities. With its focus clearly directed at the pedagogical needs of bicultural students and the educators who must meet those needs, the program offers hope in the face of despair—hope that we, as educators, will be able to transform our schools and, in so doing, meet the needs of the rapidly expanding bicultural student population in the public schools. The time has come to stop blaming the students, their parents, their communities, and their cultures, and to begin to assess the role that the schools have played in the perpetuation of the underachievement of bicultural students in this country. Hence, through participation in the Bicultural Development Program, teachers are expected to engage in the world as transformative intellectuals in a counter-hegemonic struggle for democracy in the schools and a genuinely emancipatory vision of life for all students.

Program Description

The Bicultural Development Program at Pacific Oaks requires all students to meet the standard requirements for a master's degree in human development, in addition to completing the specific coursework and practicum that constitute the preparation for the program. The standard requirements include courses in human development covering the entire life cycle. Here, students study all the major developmental theorists, including Erikson, Freud, Piaget, Maslow, and others. All students are also required to take "Social and Political Contexts" (see below), a class that carefully examines the impact of class, race, culture, and gender on development.

The foundation for the Bicultural Development Program curriculum has been built specifically on the theory of biculturalism, cultural democracy, and critical pedagogy presented in this book. Each course incorporates specific aspects of the theoretical framework and examines them with respect to the student's experiences within a context of critical dialogue. The primary goal is to prepare teachers to create critically democratic environments where bicultural students are able to participate openly, discuss their experiences freely, and develop their voice genuinely through critical interaction and dialogue with both the instructor and their fellow students. Students in the program are challenged to discover who they are in terms of their own biases and limitations, and to develop an awareness of the impact of these on their practice.

The Curriculum

The curriculum requirements for the program include the courses described below.[1] The descriptions are those found in the

Pacific Oaks College catalogue. They are presented here because they are often the determining factor for students in deciding to enroll in the Pacific Oaks program.

Social and Political Contexts of Human Development. This course explores socialization and the creation of knowledge about human development as a function of the interactions between the individual and the multileveled, social-political contexts of society. Gender, class, race, culture, disability, and sexual preference are addressed. Students are challenged to examine the specific influences on their own growth and perceptions of human behavior, the historical contexts within which specific theories of human development were created, and the impact of institutional oppression on human service programs for children and adults. Students are expected to define their personal ethics within the context of contemporary society, to relate the issues raised to their lives, and to search for creative, professional responses to inequality and bias.

Development of Bicultural Children. This course specifically focuses on a framework of bicultural development as it compares with monocultural development theories. The pertinent issues and major social, political, and economic influences that play an important role in shaping the development of bicultural children are explored. Culture and cognition, bilingualism, the biculturation process, and cultural psychological dynamics as they relate to personality development and identity formation are examined with respect to the pedagogical needs of bicultural students.

Working with Bicultural Children. This course examines methodological issues as they relate to working effectively with bicultural children. Learning theory and motivational concepts based on research with bicultural/bicognitive children are examined. Bicultural curriculum and bilingual program components are discussed. Students are required to participate in three on-site classroom observations in distinct bicultural and/or bilingual settings. Particular emphasis is placed on students integrating their understanding of the theoretical principles related to bicultural development and critical pedagogy into an effective bicultural educational practice.

Cross-cultural Mores and Values. This course is designed to consider and present a conceptual framework for review and incorporation of sociocultural factors into communication theories and practices. Specific cultural content and sociopolitical constraints on human development are examined. The importance of racial/ethnic identity is highlighted as the core of one's identity for understanding diagnostic assessment and the realizations of successful interrelations. The objective of the course is to develop knowledge of and openness and sensitivity to cultural differences.

Sociolinguistics: Issues of Language and Culture. The course explores the development of language within its social-cultural context and its implications as one of the most powerful transmitters of culture. The significant role of language as a tool of social control and/or empowerment is discussed. Particular emphasis is placed on theories of bilingualism and literacy and their relationship to bicultural development. The notion of bicultural students finding their voice is also considered within the context of American society.

Racism and Human Development. The class presents a psychosocial approach with respect to developing the antiracist consciousness and behavior necessary to work constructively with children in a racially and culturally diverse society. In a supportive environment, students are challenged to explore:

1. concepts of ethnocentrism, victim-blaming, cultural pluralism, and the dynamics of interpersonal and institutional racism;
2. the impact of racism on educational and human services programs and the role of social sciences in creating and perpetuating myths about human development;
3. the impact of racism on personal attitudes and practices;
4. new research and approaches to working with culturally diverse communities; and
5. development of skills for implementing nonracist human services work and promoting social change.

Issues of sexism and classism are also considered in relation to racism.

Theory of Cultural Democracy. The seminar focuses on the work of Manuel Ramirez and Alfredo Castaneda and their principle of cultural democracy as it relates to the educational process of bilingual and bicultural children. The research is closely examined, and the literature review of their work is presented for critical discussion. In addition, a critical model of cultural democracy is also introduced.

Implications of Parenting Bicultural Children. The seminar focuses on parenting styles as they relate specifically to the raising of bicultural children. Bicultural childrearing practices are compared with those of monocultural parents in the United States. Social, political, and economic issues that, in particular, influence bicultural parenting styles are discussed, and the cultural values related to specific bicultural parenting attitudes and behaviors are examined.

Freire's Model and Its Implications for Bicultural Educators. Paulo Freire's pedagogical framework is carefully defined and closely examined. Particular emphasis is placed on the mutual learning process of student and teacher and the significance of utilizing a dialogical method for creating effective democratic learning environments. The implications of Freire's work as it relates to the development of an effective critical bicultural educational approach is extensively discussed.

Practicum: Bicultural Development. The primary purpose of this practicum is for the student to observe, assess, evaluate, and gain hands-on experience in a bicultural educational/community setting. The student is expected to participate in a fieldwork placement for no fewer than three hour per week, in addition to classroom time.

Master's Project. All students completing the Bicultural Development Program are required to execute a research project that pertains to some specific area of bicultural development. Students are encouraged to focus on participatory and action-oriented research approaches that support emancipatory and transformative results.

The Faculty

The first coordinator for the Bicultural Development Program is a Puerto Rican woman. Three other instructors also teach in the program: two are Black; one is White. The coordinator and faculty are responsible for the majority of the design, curriculum, research, teaching, and outreach aspects of the program. The coordinator functions as advisor and master's committee chairperson for all students in the program. In addition, the ethnic and class composition of the faculty closely approximates that of the students enrolled in the program. This has proven very effective, particularly with respect to the issue of voice and the students' ability to identify with faculty members and see them as role models.

Class Requirements

In addition to extensive reading assignments, all classes require students to keep a *reflection journal* in which they document their ongoing experiences, impressions, insights, concerns, conflicts, and questions that may surface during the course of a semester. The journals are read weekly by instructors, and comments are made that function to affirm, support, and often challenge the students' views. This process assists students in developing their critical thinking skills and their writing competence. It also serves as an ongoing individual dialogue between student and teacher.

All students are also required to plan, develop, execute, and evaluate *action projects* related to the course content, which serve to demonstrate the student's ability to integrate competently the principles and theory with their practice. Action projects must be counter-hegemonic and are often done on topics related to literacy, curriculum development, textual and visual material content analysis, cultural activities in the classroom, in-service workshops for teachers on cultural issues, or any other areas considered important to meeting the pedagogical needs of bicultural communities. Students are expected to submit written project reports and make oral class presentations on their work. When possible, students are encouraged to work together in collaborative efforts.

Students are also required to demonstrate a serious engagement with the subject matter discussed in each class. This is done by way of both *small-group dialogues* and *class discussions*. Small groups are made up of 5–6 students who meet weekly for approximately forty-five minutes to engage in dialogue together about the class topic for the week. The small groups receive specific questions to discuss, based on the topic or readings and how it relates to their own lived experiences. Following the small-group dialogues, the class lecture and large-group dialogue take place, which then incorporate the students' small-group work. This has been found to be an excellent way for students to discover their own voices as they work to develop an understanding of a critical educational discourse.

Through the process of dialogue, all students have an opportunity to affirm, resist, negotiate, and challenge critically the thoughts and ideas shared by others, as well as their own. It is important to note that students are not expected to speak at all times, but rather to examine openly and critically the issues raised by both the instructor and their fellow classmates in relation to their own experiences, and ultimately to demonstrate their ability to participate in a process of reflection, critique, dialogue, and action—namely praxis.

Student Evaluations

Students are evaluated on the basis of all of the above criteria. In addition, they participate in the process of their final evaluations by submitting both a self-evaluation and a class evaluation. Here, students are asked to identify their strengths and their difficulties, as well as what the class has contributed to their development and what they have contributed as members of the group. All of this information is then considered by the instructor when writing the final semester evaluation that documents the student's progress, competencies, and areas for further improvement. Written evaluations for students at Pacific Oaks take the place of the meritocratic letter-grade system used in most educational institutions.

A CRITICAL BICULTURAL PEDAGOGY IN ACTION

In order to provide a better sense of how a critical bicultural framework functions within the dynamics of the classroom, the "Social and Political Contexts in Human Development" course will be discussed here in a bit more detail. Since one of the most important areas of competency for teachers of bicultural students is the ability to deal effectively with issues of diversity, this course is generally one of the first a student enrolls in when she or he declares the Bicultural Development Program as an academic objective. In this respect, the "Social and Political Contexts" class serves a diagnostic function in assessing the needs of students who enter the program. During the fifteen weeks of the course, students' attitudes and values surface constantly and in many ways. This phenomenon literally permits the teacher to see where students are with respect to differences in culture, race, gender, and class. This is best observed in the willingness of each student to engage with the course content through participation in group dialogues, weekly journal entries, and individual discussions with the teacher.

From the moment students step into the classroom, they are introduced to the principles of a critical discourse. This begins with an introduction to the primary purpose of the course—a purpose that is linked directly to a greater political project of social transformation. This transformative political project is identified in terms of both individual and social emancipatory interests. Hence, from the beginning, the dialectical relationship between the student as an individual and a social agent in the world is considered essential to the content and process of the class experience.

Students are informed that they will be accountable for what they do and say as participants within the social context of the class. Hence, what they do and say becomes as much "text" as what they read or hear in the teacher's lectures or class dialogues. This is discussed within a critical educational framework accepting of the notion that all thoughts, attitudes, words, and consequent actions of an individual are clearly informed by a set of values and assumptions functioning both at a conscious and unconscious level. Further, emphasis is placed on the importance and consequence that this perspective has on the educational process of the class. This is important since, generally speaking, most of the thoughts, attitudes, and values that individuals possess with respect to classism, sexism, and racism are found in the deep structures and sedimented layers of the personality, rather than at the level of full conscious awareness. Students must thus come to understand how this characteristic, in particular, is responsible for the pervasive perpetuation of different forms of oppression in our society. Further, the class places strong emphasis on the fact that *all* people, regardless of cultural origin, suffer from these forms of conflicts and contradictions, which must ultimately surface and be exposed to the conscious mind if some form of genuine transformation is to result from the work of the program's participants.

The issue of personal and social responsibility is reinforced constantly in the classroom, in order to support the development of students' awareness of themselves as social agents. Each class session is relegated to the dimension of an actual lived experience, rather than allowed to become only a suspended, academic moment in time. In essence, the class is presented as an institutional experience in which the students are all social actors. How they themselves respond to the course content and dialogue has much to teach us about who the students really are in the world, both as individuals and social beings.

Another important discussion revolves around the notion of power and power relations as a key construct in any discussion of culture, race, gender, and class. Hence, students are challenged to consider critically their own personal views of power, and how they have learned to perceive power and power relationships as they do. Consistently throughout the course of the semester, the dynamics of power are questioned and discussed. This is done as much in relation to what students themselves express as it is done in terms of the values that the class content addresses through selected books, articles, films, and lectures.

The manner in which student experiences are integrated into this process is readily apparent in the responses of several students to the issue of culture. The section on culture provides students with the opportunity to participate in small-group dialogue, in which they work together to reflect on and critique their definitions of culture. This is followed by a lecture and class dialogue that examines culture as both a seen and unseen phenomenon strongly influenced by the existing power relations within the social milieu, where cultural beings must live, work, love, and survive. Students are then asked to reflect on and critique their own culture and what values inform their personal views of the world. Examples of how students often respond to this assignment are presented below.

The first example is of a Chinese woman who has been in the United States for approximately six months. She is the daughter of a businessman who now lives in Hong Kong. As a recent immigrant to the United States, she is struggling to understand how to survive in this country. Some of her issues in the class are also related to the stereotypes she holds of bicultural communities. (These are often points of discussion among students.) On one occasion, this student is challenged when she states that "Black people should work harder if they don't want to be oppressed." In another class discussion, she openly admits she is "very afraid of Black people" because her father was assaulted by a Black man on one of his visits to the United States. These generalizations are discussed within the context of both individual and social power. This student and the other class members are asked to reflect on and critique two specifically relevant questions: (1) What are the consequences if our teaching practice is informed by a set of values that places the major responsibility for social oppression on members of subordinate groups? (2) If a White man had assaulted the father, would she be afraid of all White people?

In addition, the student here has to reflect a great deal on how her culture comes into play as she attempts to integrate into a culturally different society. She describes this struggle as follows:

I am a Chinese woman. I grew up in mainland China. I identify myself with my culture which has been existing for about 5,000 years. It values conformity to groups, obedience to elderly, and authority. Also it emphasizes the importance of family life, personal relationships, and cooperation with each other. To live harmoniously with one's inner world is the foundation of all the values we have. I learned these values, believe these values, and follow these values in my daily life.

When I moved to the U.S. I was shocked very much by the culture. It is big, and highly industrialized. It values independence, competition, individualization, achievement, as well as material—money. I am confused since my first day here. I don't know what kind of values I should pick up. I want to maintain the values I've learned in my childhood but I find that most of them don't seem to work in such an individualized society. My friends blamed me of not willing to change. Sometimes I myself would doubt whether I was trying to do something that was wrong. I found that when I started doubting myself, I felt lost. (student's journal, September 1988)

This student's conflicts are very much a part of her learning process in the class. Her experiences over the course of the semester serve as a powerful example of the immigrant biculturation process and the often painful contradictions students of color must face when confronted with mainstream values that conflict with their primary cultural perspectives. Through her engagement with the class content, lectures, journal work, and class dialogues, she is able to begin to understand and confront the conflicts and contradictions that function to interfere with her process of empowerment as an immigrant to this country. In her last journal entry she writes,

I've never been in a class like this before. It is exciting and painful. However, it ends good. I never believed I could find the strength in myself. I feel I understand better how to work with the conflict of my culture in America. I believe I understand better people of color too. I don't feel so scared anymore. I am now more aware that I am not helpless. (student's journal, December 1988)

Another student is an Anglo-American woman in her mid-twenties. She grew up in an all-White middle-class neighborhood and was not exposed to people of color until ten years ago, when she moved to California from the Midwest to attend nursing school at the University of Southern California. Initially, her perspective reflects a view that is quite common among most White students when they first enter the class. When asked to write about her cultural identity she states,

When asked to identify myself culturally and what this means, I just have to say I have no cultural identity. I am an American but I don't really feel that I have any culture to speak of. I don't really think culture is something I have ever thought very much about in my life.

I was raised to be a good person and to respect others for who they were as individuals. I never really care what culture people come from because we are all human beings and all the same. I think we all have the opportunity to succeed if we work hard enough. This is what seems to really make the difference. (September 1988)

On a number of occasions, this student is challenged in her small group and in class dialogues about her belief that all human beings are the same and about the victim-blaming attitudes she expresses when discussing the social condition of people of color. She strongly argues that "there are equal rights in America" and that, "if anyone really wants to succeed, all they have to do is get an education." Here, she and the class are asked to reflect on and critique these two questions: (1) What is the relationship between the distribution of power and economic resources in society, and the educational opportunities available to different groups? (2) What is the possible function of perpetuating the myth of the American Dream in spite of the gross inequities reflected in statistical comparisons of White men to women or people of color in the United States?

This student struggles throughout the first half of the semester to stretch her limited concept of culture and develop a better understanding of culture as it relates to the relations of power that exist in the United States. Through her constant participation in a process of reflection, dialogue, and critique, she begins to overcome her defensiveness and becomes more able to face, in a critical and thoughtful manner, the contradictions and conflicts inherent in her beliefs and practices. Her final journal entry reflects the growth she has made during the semester:

At moments, this class has been very difficult for me, but I can also say it has changed my life. If I had to describe the things I have gotten from this class they would be: (1) I now realize the depth with which racism permeates our society; (2) I now recognize the economic repression that exists in America today; and (3) I now want to work to generate change in the things that touch my life and will in the future. But I also know I still have a lot to learn about all these things. (student's journal, December 1988)

The last example is a middle-aged Black woman who was raised in a very poor segregated community in Louisiana. She came to California when her husband was drafted by the army and stationed at Ford Ord. She has lived in Watts for almost twenty years and has worked as a preschool teacher with the Head Start program for seventeen years. At the beginning of the semester, she sits quietly and seldom speaks up in the large group. In one of her first journal entries, she writes,

> I am a Black woman and I grew up in the South. There was never any question in my mind about who I am. I am and will always be Black and I know that wherever I go that's how people see me. It feels funny writing or talking about this in a college class because this has never seemed to matter in any other class I ever been in.
>
> I grew up in a very close-knit Baptist family where we all helped one another. I think this is why sometimes I have a hard time with White people because they seem so selfish to me. I usually don't say much about it because I don't want to have any trouble with them. I don't really think White folks can understand why sometimes I feel so angry. Anyway, sometimes I think it's just better to live and let live. (student's journal, September 1988)

Although this student remains silent during the first six weeks of the class, her voice becomes active when the class begins to discuss the issue of cultural oppression and racism. As part of this section, students view *Ethnic Notions,* a historical film on Black caricatures in the United States and the role they have served in perpetuating the status quo.[2] While most of the White students in the class respond to the film with some level of sensitivity, there are a few who are very critical of the film and feel resentment about what they define as all Whites having to be held accountable for the racist acts others perpetuated in the past. Some even argue that "things have really gotten better," and that they feel it might even cause more harm to be focusing on "the negative things that happened in the past."

The once-quiet student then angrily retorts, "Things may look better to you because you're White and middle-class, but maybe you should come to my neighborhood in Watts. Things there are still a mess. And everything you saw in the film has something to do with who I am, and I resent you trying to make it seem like everything is okay now." This leads to a multitude of issues for reflection and critique within the class, particularly with respect to how Whites and people of color can come to understand better the differences that exist between the way individuals and groups from the dominant culture versus subordinate cultures respond to the historical impact of cultural oppression and racism. The student's response represents the beginning of her willingness to speak publicly from the context of her bicultural voice. In her journal entry following this particular class session, she states,

> I don't know where to start. I *never* reacted in a class meeting like I did that night. Before I knew it, I was putting out exactly what I was feeling, and ready to take on whatever came after. One thing I didn't feel was any shame or fear. My feelings were out there. I must admit I am wondering how it's going to go with the class next time. But I couldn't just sit there and not speak up anymore. I'm always trying not to get so angry at White people, but things were messed up when I was young and they're still messed up.
>
> I think maybe being angry and letting White people know may not be so bad after all. I feel it was good for me to finally say what was on my mind all this time. I'm not sure where the courage came from, but I felt my inner power. Also it made me realize that I always act two ways. When I'm with my own people, I feel I can be who I am, but when I'm around Whites I feel like I can't be myself. It's like play-acting sometimes. It's awful that we have to live this way in order to survive. This has got to change. (student's journal, November 1988)

These examples of student responses illustrate well how students' lived experiences are integrated into the class content and process in very productive and constructive ways. In each of these examples it is not difficult to see how the student's responses serve not only to assist the individual student in her personal and theoretical understanding of the issues, but also to contribute to the education of her fellow students. Through a critical bicultural framework, students truly find the conditions required to explore issues of diversity, as they explore the nature of educational practices within a context of cultural democracy.

BEYOND OBJECTIVES: AN EVALUATION OF THE BICULTURAL DEVELOPMENT PROGRAM

This section will look at the results of a program evaluation process that integrates the voices of students and their experiences in the program as the major criteria for measuring success. This critical evaluation process has been utilized in place of the instrumentalized program objectives so often used in traditional program evaluations.

The Bicultural Development Program is evaluated by means of a process that includes *class evaluations* written by students and a *program evaluation student questionnaire* that is completed by all graduating students. The class evaluation was designed to give students a voice in the evaluation of the teacher and the class, as well as to provide an opportunity for students to address any concerns or difficulties they may have experienced. The program evaluation student questionnaire was designed to serve as an exit interview for the purpose of assessing the success of the program, based on the responses of students who have actually completed the program. The questionnaire includes the following questions:

1. Why did you select the Bicultural Development Program at Pacific Oaks College?
2. What have you gained from the program?
3. How has it improved your work with bicultural children and their families?
4. What personal changes have you undergone as a result of your participation in this program?
5. What institutional changes have you been directly or indirectly involved in supporting as a result of the knowledge you have gained from this program?
6. What do you consider to be the most unique qualities found in this program?
7. In what ways do you believe that your participation in this program has empowered you?
8. Other comments or suggestions?

The following are responses taken directly from the program evaluation student questionnaires, along with excerpts from reflection journals, self-evaluations, and class evaluations. Rather than diffuse or dilute the impact of the students' own voices, the responses are presented here as written. They represent those responses given by students that most closely illustrate the overall reaction of students to the Bicultural Development Program.

1. Why did you select the Bicultural Development Program at Pacific Oaks College?

- Coming from a different culture and assimilating into a different cultural world was a long process for me. I always thought that with my own experiences and the knowledge that I would gain, I could be an effective teacher for bicultural children.

- I felt the program was unique enough to set me apart from others in the field. It would open career doors for me in the educational and entertainment field as a bicultural consultant.

- The subject was of personal interest to me in that it would enhance my self-development and help me better prepare my own children and the children I teach.

- I took the class entitled "Social and Political Contexts" and rediscovered my ethnic identity which I had submerged since 1965 when I moved to California from Hawaii. I found that piece to the puzzle that is my life and reconnected and began to feel the pride of my culture again. I wanted to learn more and help others who had lost their culture and the young ones keep theirs.

- I selected this program because I am a White teacher in a bilingual classroom and I needed help understanding what the kids really needed.

- I was originally interested in this program because my future husband is Chinese and I wanted to learn as much as I can to be sensitive to him, his family, and eventually to our children, as well as to understand the implications of raising bicultural/biracial children.

- Being a person of color myself, I wanted to develop a knowledge of various issues related to culture so it would broaden my awareness of how others learn and live. This way I could better understand how to work with others who are culturally different.

- Because I work and live in the inner city and work mainly with Black and Hispanic children and families.

- With the changing demographics in California, this is a professional credential that will become more valuable as we near the year 2000.

- About three years ago, we had an *International Day* at our Headstart program and we asked each family to bring something from their cultures and the things they brought were foods, clothing, dance, and artifacts. After all the festivities were over, I felt that the true meaning wasn't there. I saw this also in the Headstart Performance Standard where we had to have multicultural materials in our classroom and what we would do was: (1) go to Olvera Street and get artifacts, (2) go to Chinatown, (3) go to Black shops in South Central LA, and then go back to the classroom and tape them on the wall and read books on people of different cultures. This usually happened prior to certain holidays: Dr. King's birthday, Cinco de Mayo, Black History Week. That seemed to be the only time we really paid attention to bicultural development. I felt we needed to do more. That's why I selected the Bicultural Development Program.

• This program offered me a new challenge, and since my occupation involves children from many cultures, I wanted to study other ideas and ways to support the empowerment of bicultural children.

• Because I am monocultural (Anglo-American) and I wanted to understand things from a perspective other than what I've been taught and what I have experienced. I am a teacher and I wanted to be more effective in creating learning experiences for the children that reflect a respect for diversity, but I didn't really know how to go about doing this.

2. What have you gained from the program?

• Insights into my own development and the lives of bicultural children in this country.

• Affirmation of my own worth and the value of my contribution to society.

• A passion to work to make things better, especially for the bicultural child.

• I learned that it was okay to hurt and feel anger at what happened to me (going underground with my culture in order to be accepted by the mainstream). This helped me to begin to see a new me and I wanted to learn more. This program gave me good background information on issues related to differences in cultural views, as well as an understanding of the White European culture.

- I have gained a multitude of knowledge in many areas. I have become more aware of myself, culturally speaking, as well as my attitudes towards people of other cultures. I have learned to understand biases, stereotypes, and racism and how to fight against them in my classroom. I have learned a lot about Black and Latino children and other bicultural children too.
- This program has given me a necessary theoretical framework as a tool in relating, understanding, and working with bicultural children. I have gotten so much practical curriculum that I have been using it in my daily work with children.
- I have learned positive ways to teach children about differences and how to deal with conflicts in the classroom. I have also learned much about cultural development and have become more comfortable and positive in my attitude when working with children of various cultural backgrounds.
- I have gained a real understanding of how to apply my knowledge of cultures and cultural diversity to my work experiences and my daily life.
- I have gained more knowledge on how to work with bicultural children and their families in an effective way.
- This program has crystallized the need to help bicultural children (as well as myself) get a clearer understanding of how important it is to provide accurate cultural information, respect for diversity, love, and support to each student no matter where they come from or their ethnicity.
- I have not only gained a broader perspective of the world, reality, and my role as a teacher, but I have also gained a totally different view of life that I had never realized or been taught before. I have gained a whole new way of thinking and teaching.

3. How has it improved your work with bicultural children and their families?

- I feel that I now have an understanding that has been strengthened by both objective information as well as subjective knowledge. I realize that it is not enough to empathize or sympathize with the struggle one feels is going on with bicultural children and their families; we must be able together to face it and name it. Then we can create solution, techniques, and methods to counteract society's negative influence.

- I am learning how to understand better and prevent cross-cultural misunderstanding. I teach a multicultural class for preschool teachers at a local junior college, and I try to help them to understand more about their children's culture and help them see that many times problems come about because of a misunderstanding of cultural differences.

- It has helped me gain a better understanding into my motives as a teacher, which I had always considered *pure*. Now I am beginning to understand my *political* role as a teacher and how to develop a better program for bicultural children.

- I don't feel so intimidated by bicultural children or adults anymore. I always thought I embraced differences, but what I used to do was only take a tourist approach to cultural differences. Now, I feel like I am informed enough to deal with bicultural communities on all levels—with children, I can specifically focus on their cognitive, social, emotional, and physical needs.

- It has given me social, political, and cultural knowledge and the critical tools necessary in my interaction with bicultural children and their families. It has improved my work with them a great deal and helped me to be a better teacher.

- It has prepared me in teaching and encouraging bicultural parents to be involved actively in their children's learning—helping parents use their expertise and knowledge of their own culture as a learning experience with materials and methods to meet the needs of their children. From this I have also learned from the families about how the process of their culture takes place and I can become more understanding of what they feel they need.

- I try to be more sensitive to their needs and I treat each child and the family with value and respect. I don't assume anything when it comes to their needs. I try to maintain a more personal contact with the families, making home visits and taking extra time to talk with the mothers when they pick up their children and volunteer in the classroom.

- I understand better that the foundation for my work must be accurate and based on real lived information when discussing bicultural children and their families. This program has opened my eyes to areas that I need to improve and how I've needed to become better educated about what really goes on. My community involvement has also taken new directions.

- For one thing, my whole concept of values has changed. I never really thought about the fact that different cultures prioritize values in different ways. And throughout my schooling in child development, it was the *individual* development that was always stressed. Now I can see the larger picture of the bicultural child in relation to the family and community, and I look at those aspects as I plan and teach.

4. What personal changes have you undergone as a result of your participation in this program?

- I have personally become a much stronger person, not willing to sit back and let someone else do it. I think I've become *politicized*—and I like the feeling.
- There is a title that I recently have begun to use concerning myself: *a women of color: a woman of substance*. I realize that I am a woman of color and it finally feels great. I realize now that I am also a person of substance in this world. Before, in denying my culture, there was an empty spot in my life, a feeling of being incomplete—without substance.
- So many things have come to mind. I see it in my work every day as a result of the classes I have taken. My attitude has become more open to the ideas of others that in the past I just rejected as *silly* or unimportant.
- I am much more critical now than I have ever been, I am constantly examining books, movies, curriculum, etc.—evaluating its appropriateness for bicultural children. I have also found the confidence and voice to share my feelings and knowledge with my family, friends, and co-workers.
- I have been able to put my own personal experiences into the context of my learning and my teaching. It has empowered and validated my values and it has broadened my perspective to overcome my own ethnocentrism and to value the differences of others.
- After taking the classes in the program, I have become involved in community programs for bicultural children to learn to read. I realize I must be involved in my work and my community to make changes.
- I am more sensitive to each family and I make a special effort to try and know the family in a more full way. I have been

able to not pre-judge any bicultural family. I now try to put myself in their place and accept their customs, traditions, and child-raising practices as part of the way they struggle to survive, and I see how we can work together for their children.

• Prior to being in the program, I really avoided getting down to knowing what I wanted to do. Here I learned to value my own experiences and understand how to work with my own ideas, thoughts, and experiences in becoming a better teacher.

• The way that I think, speak, teach, and behave has changed. I have *a lot* more conflicts with my family, friends, and associates because of the ways I've changed. But it's okay with me because I know I now understand a lot more than I used to about myself as a White woman and about my work with bicultural children.

• Being part of the Bicultural Program has been one of the most, if not the most, personally satisfying experiences of my development as a teacher. I know I am becoming better prepared to move effectively to meet the needs of my bicultural students.

• Now, as a result of this program, I am pursuing a degree and have learned more about myself and the children with whom I work. It has helped me to discover my desire to look at holidays and how they are unfairly related to real life in the curriculum and the damages that result to bicultural communities.

5. What institutional changes have you been directly or indirectly involved in supporting as a result of the knowledge you have gained from this program?

• I was a member of a group of parents who worked to remove a principal at my son's elementary school because of his racist behavior. We worked with city officials to remove a person who treated parents, teachers, and pupils as his personal property—with no rights of their own. A problem which had persisted for over eight years was corrected in six months through our collective struggle.

• My teaching has definitely changed. I am no longer able to just sit quietly when negative racial comments or misunderstandings of cultural differences arise. I am closely monitoring these things in my school and working to make definite suggestions for next semester.

- I have become very involved with the bilingual committee at my school which is pushing for changes in our program. And although we're not winning any popularity contests at the present time, we are persevering in our fight to change the way bicultural children are educated at our school.

- I am currently in the process of working on implementing an anti-bias curriculum in my classroom at a center that claims to be practicing it, but no real effort is taking place to bring it about in the classroom practice. I am training my staff on institutional racism, language use, book selection, holidays, etc. in order for everyone to be more sensitive to bicultural children and their families.

- I have been involved with parent education meetings and I am a member of our school curriculum committee. We have been able to bring more children of color to the school and have worked to have bicultural education and an anti-bias curriculum as part of the school's philosophy and practice.

- How I approach my work with parents has changed. I am more sensitive and conscious of people's cultures and their real-life struggles. I am more open to different lifestyles and how to better serve families from various cultures, economic backgrounds, and different languages.

- I have been involved in changes at the site where I am a Head Teacher. We have about one-third Blacks, Hispanics, and Asian children and families. The first and most important change that I have been involved in with staff is stressing the importance of not being demeaning to children when they are in a group speaking their native language. It's important not to yell at the children, insisting they speak English and prohibiting them from speaking their native language—as many teachers used to do. It's been difficult for most teachers because they have been trained to not let children speak their native language. But I just keep at it.

- Within my job, I have encouraged people to question or to demand changes when the administration acts unfairly. I personally have confronted the administration with a formal complaint. I don't think I would have done this prior to this program. It has helped me improve conditions at this time.

- My preschool program in my classroom has totally changed. I have changed my role as a teacher in order to take more responsibility for creating the atmosphere through my curriculum in my classroom that is culturally democratic.

• In my work with student teachers, I developed a program for them that is accepting and sensitive to all cultural groups but that also challenges ideas and practices that are unfair in any situation. This was something that was missing before.

• I now teach a community college class on anti-bias curriculum where we look at our own biases as teachers and we attempt to challenge and change these biases.

• I organized *Freedom in Education*—a support group for kindergarten teachers. The group meets once a week and dialogues on liberatory educational practices for young children. We are working on some basic curriculum changes together and discuss how they work with bicultural children in our classrooms.

6. What do you consider to be the most unique qualities found in this program?

• The materials used, such as books, articles, workshops, field studies, etc., are of the highest quality, thought-provoking, and involving to all students. It is challenging, but the curriculum is structured in such a way that each class builds on the previous one, with obvious growth in the students.

• First of all, having a woman of color heading this program. You need a person who has *been there*. The personal experiences that have been shared by students as well cannot be duplicated in any book learning. The faculty is tough on issues and not afraid to challenge a student to think!

• The teaching staff and their unique lifestyles. They weren't teaching something they didn't practice in their own work and their own lives. The fieldwork was so interesting, and listening and sharing with other students who had different ideas—learning how they had arrived to certain ways of looking at the world helped me to learn so much about what I have not experienced.

• I believe this program is unique in that the information and materials shared are so applicable in many areas of life—not just our teaching. There's not just one or two jobs for which this degree prepares you, but rather a whole way of interpreting life and all the people you meet and work with along the way.

- The most unique quality that I found in this program has been the nature of teaching the classes.
- It helps a person develop a more strong self-image, and it encourages students of color to maintain and honor their culture and to be proud of who we are, where we came from, our heritage, and what we have to contribute to the world.
- You are able to go out and do community work and get hands-on experience with people of color and bicultural families. I have found it to be more educational and human than any other form of education I have received. Even going into different communities just to observe families and children in community markets and comparing the differences in foods eaten taught us more about what it means to be bicultural in this country.
- The ability to get to true concerns, learn how to help and accomplish a task that we are concerned about in an honest and skilled manner. Doing instead of just talking—*ACTION*. There were real experiences, the real world, not faking.
- The fact that you must validate humanity and experiences that are usually neglected, negated, or labeled *deviant* in our institutions by the ruling class and the dominant culture.
- The classes were always *excellent*. I always leave feeling more powerful and optimistic about myself and my work with bicultural children. It gives me hope.
- The faculty has been an inspiration to my work and to my life. I have gained so many insights on how to deal with issues that I must face with Whites when dealing with the needs of bicultural children. This program has really prepared me to do this successfully, and I don't think I would have learned this in other programs.

7. In what ways do you believe that your participation in this program has empowered you?

- It has armed me with an impressive amount of information which helps me to make my case for the importance of addressing and acknowledging the value of biculturalism.
- The program has given me the tools for making presentations which will move others intellectually and emotionally to understand themselves and people of color more honestly.

- I feel such a sense of freedom and so much pride in my culture now, that *watch out* to whomever I come in contact with! I wish I could find the words to tell you how much growth has come about in me in one short year. It's been scary but definitely exciting.

- There isn't one day that something I learned in these classes doesn't pop up in my everyday practice—having the skills to deal with bicultural children and their families makes me feel definitely empowered.

- I feel empowered by the fact that this is a new field of study and that there is such a high need for this information and this perspective in so many areas. The first few groups of us to graduate are really *pioneers* in this program, and knowing we have something to offer that is really positive is validating to me in my work as a teacher.

- I feel that my thoughts, experiences, and my values have been validated, respected, and listened to. I find that my voice is getting stronger and I can no longer ignore racial abuses. I also have come to understand how our values influence what we do. I feel a greater commitment to speak my voice, to challenge and understand others. I have found the hope that I lacked before in my work and my struggle for social change.

- Being able to be more open about my feelings has helped to empower me. Also to care and respect those who may not understand the way I feel or my culture or the pressure or rejection I have felt from the dominant culture—this has helped me to maintain my integrity as a person of color and to free me from always feeling like a victim.

- It has made me more outspoken. I don't just sit back and let other teachers or people say and do things that oppress people of color where I work. When anyone comes in with the attitude of *those people,* I can speak up and say, *Look, don't say those people. They have a culture and you don't know what they have been through. So let's talk about it together before you start victim-blaming without knowing what's happening.*

- The program has empowered me to go directly to a person that I have a difference with, whether academic or to help a student. Example: A young Black child seemed to be having difficulty reading. He seemed to be having problems focusing and I talked to his teacher to offer suggestions. I thought he might be dyslexic.

But the teacher had not even noticed him more than to call him
a *trouble-maker*. After some dialogue with the teacher, she began
to offer him a guided program and he is improving. In the past
I would have felt awkward confronting the teacher.

 • One of the most important ways that the program helped me
to feel empowered was through helping me accept *all* of my
humanity—my strengths and my limitations. I was validated for
all my parts—not only my mind and my body, but my emotions
and my spirit as well. I heard this in each class. It was a very
powerful and emotional experience for me. I finally felt whole.

 • I've learned about confrontation. It has to be truthful. I don't
have to be afraid anymore. I've learned more about critical thinking just in this program than I had learned in the past twenty
years. I've also learned a lot about facing up to bitter truths, contradictions, and the nature of the insidious oppression that affects
all of us. But more than this, I have learned how to confront it
and how to work with others to change it.

 • I have embraced this new knowledge not only in my work
with bicultural children but in my personal life. The process of
dialogue has empowered me to better know and trust myself and
my own experiences.

 • I am empowered to trust my own perceptions. This makes
the world a much safer place in which to risk. It is not always
easy, but I know there is more I can come to understand. I can
encourage others as I have been encouraged because I know
change is possible. I am thankful for that understanding.

8. Other comments or suggestions?

 • Such a program should receive support from the College so
that it may grow.

 • This program has made a real advocate out of me. We need
more programs like this, and I truly believe that anyone who goes
through this program will come out a much changed person for
the better.

 • The reason I am in this program is because of the teaching,
which motivated us to think, to talk, to act, to do problem-solving,
and gave us a broadened perspective to help us better understand
how to work with others, particularly for me as a bicultural teacher.

- I believe that everyone involved in working with people of color on a daily basis should enroll in Bicultural Development Program courses. It will give them a new insight on how others live in this society. It has inspired me to continue learning more.
- I leave with a head and a heart full of knowledge that I will carry forever, wherever I go—wherever I teach.
- Student teachers should have to participate in a practical assignment that jolts them into looking at the realities of people of color in this society. Students need opportunities to observe and participate in real-life activities such as we have received in this program. The films and critique have also been helpful.
- This program was the best thing that I've ever been involved in. It has helped me to change and to understand in ways that I never imagined nor expected. It has provided very important role models for me.

IN CONCLUSION

It is important to note that the Pacific Oaks College Bicultural Development Program has been specifically designed with full consideration of the educational needs of students who are both adults and teachers in Southern California, the faculty's strengths and limitations, the available resources, and the institutional requirements for granting a degree. This program is not meant to serve as a recipe, nor is it expected that the program will be duplicated identically elsewhere. Rather, it is meant to serve as an example of a relatively new program that was built specifically on the critical bicultural educational framework posited in this book. A similar teacher education program in another part of the country would share the basic theoretical constructs but might rearrange the curriculum or requirements in a very different manner, depending on the needs of the student population, the faculty, the resources available, and institutional mandates.

Most importantly, this text represents an effort to define how a critical bicultural framework—based on the principles of critical pedagogy, cultural democracy and biculturalism—can inform a critical bicultural education practice. Although this work is not meant to function as a definitive teacher preparation model in critical bicultural education, it is meant to provide the critical tools to assist educators of bicultural children in carrying out an assessment of current theories and practices. But further, this work embodies a transformative vision; it seeks, above all, an educational experience that will truly prepare bicultural students to share equally in the remaking of our world—genuinely dedicated, in theory and practice, to the principles of democracy, social justice, and human rights.

NOTES

1. Each unit of course credit at Pacific Oaks College is equivalent to a minimum of one hour of teacher-contact time per week.

2. See Chapter 2, note 3.

BIBLIOGRAPHY

Adorno, T. 1973. *Prisms*. London: Neville Spearman.

Anyon, J. 1979. "United States History Textbooks and Ideology: A Study of Curriculum Content and Social Interests." *Harvard Educational Review* 46: p. 49–59.

———. 1980. "Social Class and the Hidden Curriculum of Work." *Journal of Education* 162: pp. 121–26.

Arblaster, A. 1987. *Democracy*. Minneapolis: University of Minnesota Press.

Aronowitz, S., and Giroux, H. 1985. *Education under Siege*. New York: Bergin & Garvey.

Blauner, R. 1972. *Racial Oppression in America*. New York: Harper & Row.

Bloom, B. 1964. *Stability and Change in Human Characteristics*. New York: Macmillan.

Boas, F. 1938. *The Mind of the Primitive Man*. New York: Macmillan.

Bowles, S., and Gintes, H. 1976. *Schooling in Capitalist America*. New York: Basic Books.

Carnoy, M. 1974. *Education as Cultural Imperialism*. New York: David McKay.

Carter, T. 1970. *Mexican Americans in School: A History of Educational Neglect*. New York: College Entrance Examination Board.

Clark, K. 1965. *Dark Ghetto: Dilemmas of Social Power*. New York: Harper & Row.

Cohen, R., et al. 1968. "The Language of the Hard Core Poor: Implications for Culture-Conflict." *American Anthropologist* 70: pp. 828–56.

Cole, M., and Scribner, S. 1974. *Culture and Thought*. New York: John Wiley & Sons.

Coleman J., et al. 1966. *Equality of Educational Opportunity*. Washington, DC: U.S. Department of Health, Education, and Welfare.

Cross, W. E. 1978. "The Thomas and Cross Models on Psychological Nigrescence: A Literature Review." *Journal of Black Psychology* 4: pp. 13–31.

Cummins, J. 1986. "Empowering Minority Students: A Framework for Intervention." *Harvard Educational Review* 56: pp. 18–36.

Daniels, J., and Houghton, V. 1972. "Jensen, Eysenck, and the Eclipse of the Galton Paradigm." In K. Richardson and D. Spears, eds., *Race and Intelligence*. Baltimore: Penguin Books.

Davies, D. 1981. *Popular Culture, Class, and Schooling*. London: Open University Press.

deAnda, D. 1984. "Bicultural Socialization: Factors Affecting the Minority Experience." *Social Work* 2: pp. 101–07.

deLone, R. 1979. *Small Futures*. New York: Harcourt Brace Jovanovich.

Dewey, J. 1916. *Democracy and Education*. New York: Free Press.

Dixon, V., and Foster, B. 1971. *Beyond Black or White*. Boston: Little Brown.

Du Bois, W. E. B. 1903. *Souls of Black Folk*. Chicago: A. C. McClurg.

Fanon, F. 1961. *Black Skins, White Masks*. New York: Grove Press.

Fay, B. 1987. *Critical Social Science*. London: Cornell University Press.

Fishman, J., and Keller, G. 1982. *Bilingual Education for Hispanic Students in the United States*. New York: Teacher's College of Columbia University.

Forester, J. 1987. *Critical Theory and Public Life*. Boston: MIT Press.

Foucault, M. 1977. *Power/Knowledge: Selected Interviews and Other Writings*. New York: Pantheon Books.

Freire, P. 1970. *Pedagogy of the Oppressed*. New York: Seabury Press.

——. 1978. *Education for Critical Consciousness*. New York: Seabury Press.

——. 1985. *The Politics of Education*. New York: Bergin and Garvey.

Freire, P., and Macedo, D. 1987. *Literacy: Reading the Word and the World*. New York: Bergin & Garvey.

Galton, F. 1869. *Hereditary Genius*. New York: Macmillan.

Gilbert, S., and Gay, G. 1985. "Improving the Success in Schools of Poor Black Children." *Phi Delta Kappan*: pp. 131–37.

Giroux, H. 1981. *Ideology, Culture, and the Process of Schooling*. Philadelphia: Temple University Press.

——. 1983. *Theory and Resistance in Education*. New York: Bergin & Garvey.

——. 1985. "Teachers as Transformative Intellectuals." *Social Education* 2: pp. 376–79.

——. 1988a. *Teachers as Intellectuals*. New York: Bergin & Garvey.

——. 1988b. *Schooling and the Struggle for Public Life*. Minneapolis: University of Minnesota Press.

——. 1990. "The Politics of Postmodernism: Rethinking the Boundaries of Race and Ethnicity." *Journal of Urban and Cultural Studies* 1: pp. 5–38.

Giroux, H., and McLaren, P. 1987. "Teacher Education as a Counter Public Sphere: Radical Pedagogy as a Form of Cultural Politics." *Philosophy and Social Criticism* 12: pp. 51–69.

Glasgow, D. 1980. *The Black Underclass*. New York: Random House, Inc.

Goldenberg, A. 1987. "Low-income Hispanic Parents' Contribution to Their First Grader Children's Word Recognition Skills." *Anthropology and Education Quarterly* 18: pp. 149–77.

Gould, S. J. 1981. *The Mismeasurement of Man*. New York: W. W. Norton.

Gramsci, A. 1971. *Selections from Prison Notebooks*. New York: International Publications.

Habermas, J. 1970. "Toward a Theory of Communicative Competence." In H. P. Dreitzel, ed., *Recent Sociology*. New York: Macmillan.

Hall, S. 1981. "Cultural Studies: Two Paradigms." In T. Bennett et al., eds., *Culture, Ideology, and Social Process*. London: Batsford Academic & Educational.

Held, D. 1980. *Introduction to Critical Theory*. London: Heinemann.

Hernandez, C., et al. 1976. *Chicanos: Social and Psychological Perspectives*. St. Louis: Mosby.

Hodge, J., et al. 1975. *Cultural Bases of Racism and Group Oppression*. Berkeley: Two Riders Press.

Hooks, B. 1989. *Talking Back*. Boston: South End Press.

Horkheimer, M. 1972. *Critical Theory: Selected Essays*. New York: Herder & Herder.

Hsu, F. 1971. *The Challenge of the American Dream: The Chinese in the United States*. Belmont, CA: Wadsworth.

Hudson, L. 1972. "The Context of the Debate." In K. Richardson and D. Spears, eds., *Race and Intelligence*. Baltimore: Penguin Books.

Jay, M. 1973. *The Dialectical Imagination*. Boston: Little Brown.

Jensen, A. 1969. "How Much Can We Boost I.Q. and Scholastic Achievement?" *Harvard Educational Review* 1: pp. 147–63.

Johnson, R. 1983. "What Is Cultural Studies Anyway?" *Angistica* 26: pp. 7–81.

Keddie, N. 1971. "Classroom Knowledge." In M. F. D. Young, ed., *Knowledge and Control*. London: Collier-Macmillan.

Kitano, H. 1969. *Japanese-Americans: The Evolution of a Subculture.* Englewood Cliffs, NJ: Prentice-Hall.

Kluckhohn, F., and Strodbeck, F. 1961. *Variations in Value Orientation.* New York: Row, Peterson.

Knowles, L., and Prewitt, K. 1969. *Institutional Racism in America.* Englewood Cliffs, NJ: Prentice-Hall.

Kozol, J. 1990. "The New Untouchables." *Newsweek,* Special Issue, pp. 48–53.

Lewis, O. 1966. "The Culture of Poverty." *Scientific American* 215: pp. 19–25.

McAdoo, H. 1977. "Family Therapy in the Black Community." *American Journal of Orthopsychiatry* 47: pp. 75–79.

McLaren, P. 1988. *Life in Schools: An Introduction to Critical Pedagogy in the Foundations of Education.* New York: Longman.

Marcuse, H. 1955. *Eros and Civilization: A Philosophical Inquiry into Freud.* Boston: Beacon Press.

Mead, M., ed. 1937. *Cooperation and Competition among Primitive Peoples.* New York: McGraw-Hill.

Memmi, A., 1965. *The Colonizer and the Colonized.* Boston: Beacon Press.

Miller, W. 1958. "Lower Class Culture as a Generating Milieu of Gang Delinquency." *Journal of Social Issues* 14: pp. 5–19.

Munroe, R., and Munroe, R. 1975. Cross-cultural Human Development. Monterey, CA: Brooks/Cole.

Moynihan, D. P. 1965. *The Negro Family: The Case for National Action.* Washington, DC: Government Printing Office.

Ogbu, J. 1978. *Minority Education and Caste: The American System in Cross-cultural Perspective.* New York: Academic Press.

Ovando, C., and Collier, V. 1985. *Bilingual and ESL Classrooms.* New York: McGraw-Hill.

Persell, C. H. 1977. *Education and Inequality.* New York: Free Press.

Phillips, C. 1979. "Rethinking the Study of Black Behavior." In *Collective Monographs I: Toward a Black Perspective in Education.* Pasadena, CA: Stage 7.

——. 1988. "Nurturing Diversity for Today's Children and Tomorrow's Leaders." *Young Children* 43: pp. 42–47.

Pialorsi, F. 1974. *Teaching the Bilingual.* Flagstaff, AZ: University of Arizona Press.

Pokewitz, T. S. 1978. "Educational Research: Values and Visions of Social Order." *Theory and Research in Social Education* 6: pp. 81–101.

Porter, J., and Washington, R. 1979. "Black Identity and Self-esteem: A Review of Studies of Black Self-concept." *Annual Review of Sociology* 5: pp. 53–74.

Ramirez, M., and Castaneda, A. 1974. *Cultural Democracy: Bicognitive Development and Education*. New York: Academic Press.

Rashid, H. 1981. "Early Childhood Education as a Cultural Transition for African-American Children." *Educational Research Quarterly* 6: pp. 55–63.

Red Horse, J., et al. 1981. "Family Behavior of Urban American Indians." In R. Dana, ed., *Human Services for Cultural Minorities*. Baltimore: University Park Press.

Richardson, K., and Spears, D. 1972. *Race and Intelligence*. Baltimore: Penguin Books.

Rist, R. 1977. *The Urban School: A Factory of Failure*. Boston: MIT Press.

Rosenbaum, J. 1976. *Making Inequality*. New York: Wiley Interscience.

Rosenthal, R., and Jacobson, L. 1968. *Pygmalion in the Classroom*. New York: Holt, Rinehart & Winston.

Ryan, W. 1976. *Blaming the Victim*. New York: Vintage Books.

——. 1981. *Equality*. New York: Pantheon Books.

Shor, I., and Freire, P. 1987. *A Pedagogy for Liberation*. New York: Bergin & Garvey.

Simon, R. 1987. "Empowerment as a Pedagogy of Possibility." *Language Arts* 64: pp. 370–89.

——. 1988. "For a Pedagogy of Possibility." *Critical Pedagogy Networker* 1: pp. 1–4.

——. 1991. *Learning Work: A Critical Pedagogy of Work Education*. New York: Bergin & Garvey.

Solis, A. 1980. "Theory of Biculturality." *Calmecac de Aztlan en Los* 1: pp. 7–12.

——. 1981. "Theory of Biculturality." *Calmecac de Aztlan en Los* 2: 36–41.

Steele, S. 1990. *The Content of Our Character*. New York: St. Martin's Press.

Suarez, C. 1978. "Values in the Development of Curriculum for Chicanos." In *Cultural Issues in Education*. San Diego, CA: National Multilingual Multicultural Materials Development Center.

Sue, S., and Sue, D. W. 1978. "Chinese-American Personality and Mental Health." *Amerasia Journal* 1: pp. 36–49.

Turner, P. 1982. *Bilingualism in the Southwest*. Flagstaff, AZ: University of Arizona Press.

Tyler, E. B. 1891. *Primitive Culture*. London: John Murray.

Valentine, C. 1971. "Deficit, Difference, and Bicultural Models of Afro-American Behavior." *Harvard Educational Review* 41: pp. 137–57.

Valverde, L. 1978. *Bilingual Education for Latinos*. Washington, DC: Association for Supervision and Curriculum Development.

Warren, S. 1984. *The Emergence of Dialectical Theory*. Chicago: University of Chicago Press.

Weiler, K. 1985. *Women Teaching for Change: Gender, Class, and Power*. New York: Bergin & Garvey.

Whorf, B. 1956. *Language, Thought, and Reality*. Boston: MIT Press.

Witkin, H., and Berry, J. 1975. "Psychological Differentiation in Cross-cultural Perspective." *Journal of Cross-cultural Psychology*, 6: pp. 4–87.

Wright, R. N. 1953. *The Outsider*. New York: Harper & Row.

INDEX

positivism, 6–8, 31, 80
power: conservative view of,
108; contradictory assumptions of, 109; culture and,
26–44; dominant, 29, 30;
hegemonic, 34, 35; human
agency, 89; knowledge and,
27, 28, 77, 89, 92; liberal view
of, 108; modes of domination,
35; reinvention of, 93; subordinate, 29, 30; and truth, 27,
28
practice/praxis, 82–84

racism, 38–42; challenging,
116–18
Ramirez, Manuel, 48, 51–53;
philosophy of cultural
democracy, 60-62
Rashid, Hakim, 53
restructuring schools, 74, 116,
123–26; classroom en-
vironments, 67, 124;
classroom relationships, 125;
redefining teacher's workday,
126
Rosenbaum, Jane, 15, 18
resistance, 42–44, 88–91;
language, 44; legacy of, 105
ruling class, 15, 31
Ryan, William, 10, 17–19

Simon, Roger, 76, 100, 106

Social Darwinism, 14, 39, 113
solidarity, 64, 121, 128
Solis, Arnoldo, 53, 54
stereotyping, 41
subjectivity, 32

teacher: authority, 107–10;
dependency on prescribed curriculum, 100; expectations,
17–19; fears of theory, 106
technocratic rationality, 7
theory: of biculturality, 53; fear
of, 106, 107; instrumental
definition, 7; language of,
104–6; and practice, 82–85
tracking and ability grouping,
15–17
transformative intellectuals, 93
truth: cultural, 78; and
knowledge, 27, 92; and
power, 27, 28

universalism, 39

Valentine, Charles, 49, 50
value free/neutral, 11, 78, 81
Valverde, Leonard, 61
victim-blaming, 2, 9, 10
voice, 39, 60, 65–68, 92, 102,
103; bicultural, 47, 60, 68–71,
97, 107; struggle for, 107

Weiler, Kathleen, 89

About the Author

ANTONIA DARDER is Assistant Professor of Education at Claremont Graduate School, Claremont, California. She has also been a guest lecturer at the Massachusetts Institute of Technology and an associate professor at Lesley College in Massachusetts. She established the first graduate program in bicultural development in the country when she taught at Pacific Oaks College in Pasadena.